Why the Eucharist Matters for Your Life

The Practical Reality

of Christ's Power & Presence

WHY THE
EUCHARIST
MATTERS
FOR YOUR LIFE

THE PRACTICAL REALITY
of CHRIST'S POWER & PRESENCE

CHRIS PADGETT

Published by The Word Among Us Press
7115 Guilford Drive, Suite 100
Frederick, Maryland 21704
www.wau.org

18 17 16 15 14   1 2 3 4 5

ISBN: 978-1-59325-259-5
eISBN: 978-1-59325-460-5

Cover design by John Hamilton Design

Made and printed in the United States of America

Library of Congress Control Number: 2014945335

CONTENTS

ACKNOWLEDGMENTS

Many thanks to the team at The Word Among Us Press. I am excited to be a part of the family. I would especially like to thank my wife, Linda, and our nine children. I am praying that they will grow in their love of Christ and one another. I suppose my greatest gifts to my children would be to love their mother entirely, faithfully, and joyfully, and to allow them to witness a broken man regularly healed by the loving presence of Jesus in the sacraments. Keep us in your prayers.

INTRODUCTION

There are many things I could have put in this little book. Just the many quotes about the Eucharist by saints would fill numerous books! Here, however, I simply wanted to look at this simple question: how does the Eucharist affect the way I live my life? Will I be more forgiving because of the Eucharist? Will I find strength in the Eucharist to be more patient, gentle, and self-controlled? Will the reception of Jesus at Mass affect my stance on political and moral issues? Yes to all of the above!

The relationship that Jesus offers to us through his constant presence in the Eucharist enables us to see the world and ourselves differently. You will discover that I didn't spend time looking at the Old Testament types that are fulfilled in the New Testament, nor did I give you an examination of the Eucharistic passages in the Gospels and St. Paul's writings. I wanted you to find an immediate connection between receiving Jesus in the Eucharist and living a holy life in difficult times. As you read the reflections, I hope you are spurred to greater love for Christ and become more open to the many different ways that he wants to be present in your day-to-day life. I hope you are encouraged, and I hope you find many ways to be Eucharistic people!

There are a number of ways for you to approach this book. It is structured so that you can use it as part of an Ignatian-style retreat over the course of forty days, so it would be perfect for Lent. (I am not implying that you will suffer because of what you read here, although if you do, there may be some spiritual fruit!) You might want to use these reflections during Eucharistic adoration. Each reflection invites you to enter into the presence of Jesus. He is already faithfully present in our lives through the Eucharist, but this book may help you become more aware of it.

You can read the whole book through from start to finish or pick and choose as you wish. May you find this book thought-provoking and helpful, because I have truly been encouraged and challenged in writing it.

Chris Padgett

PART ONE:
EUCHARISTIC LOVE

BELOVED OF GOD

*God's unconditional love is expressed
most tangibly in the Eucharist.*

One morning at Mass, I was struck by the realization that our Father looks at each of us and says to us what he said to Jesus: "This is my beloved child, with whom I am well pleased" (cf. Matthew 17:5). We don't often think that God might be filled with joy at the sight of us. Our failures and frustrations seem to be glaring reasons for him to be distant and disappointed, and yet he is pleased. Why? Because we are his.

This is difficult for us to understand, but God wanted us, fought for us, and paid the ultimate price in order to be in a relationship with us! Even when we make mistakes, God's love for us is unbending and unwavering. To be loved just as we are, sinful and imperfect, seems so countercultural because—unfortunately—our culture's comprehension of love is conditional. God's love is not. He is pleased with us even when we are not pleased with ourselves. Our God loves us even when we struggle to love ourselves.

In his book *Back to Virtue*, Peter Kreeft describes *agape* as "the love that kissed the traitor Judas, suffered the soldiers' slaps and sneers, and prayed, 'Father, forgive them, for they know not what they do.'"[1] The phrase "the love that kissed the traitor Judas" stood out to me. Think of a small child's resistance at being kissed when he isn't interested. He will squirm, wiggle, or do anything to avoid it. Jesus could have easily turned away from Judas, who approached and greeted him with a kiss. This was Judas' moment of betrayal, but as a friend, Jesus genuinely accepted and received that kiss and, as Kreeft suggests, even returned it.

Simply put, Jesus loves us even when we betray him, even when we deny him, even when we run from him, and even when we don't recognize him. He expresses this most tangibly when we celebrate the Eucharist. How many times have we walked into church acting as if we love Jesus when our actions have proved otherwise? How often have we drifted off into a spiritual slumber after Jesus specifically asked us to watch and pray? Haven't we fled when difficulties surfaced, just as the disciples did so long ago? Have we not in other moments pretended that we are not actually associated with Jesus, just so that we could avoid mockery or difficulties with others?

The Lord loves us when our attempts to love him fail. He loves us when we worry about what others will think if we make the Sign of the Cross in public, and he loves us when we carelessly indulge in selfish behavior rather than in selfless acts. Jesus, knowing all of our flaws, still willingly died for the sins we commit, not only against others, but even against himself.

We have a lot to learn about the intimacy to which Jesus invites us at every Mass. I can imagine that most of us, on more occasions than we would like to admit, have gone through the motions on a Sunday morning during the celebration of the Eucharist, thinking only of the many things that are going on in our lives. However, even in the times at Mass when we are more concerned with a football game or a work-related issue, Jesus still willingly and entirely comes to embrace us.

I wonder if we could have that type of understanding towards the people in our lives who seem to intentionally or unintentionally ignore us. What if we embraced and loved those who were not really focused on us during a conversation, or even those who were looking around the room trying to find someone else to talk to while we were sharing a personal story with them? What if we remembered that the love that Jesus has for us is the kind of love that we can offer to others? It would change the world!

Prayer Starter: Do I believe that Jesus really loves me unconditionally? What obstacles in my life might be preventing me from fully accepting the love that he has for me?

[1] Peter Kreeft, *Back to Virtue* (San Francisco: Ignatius Press, 2009), p. 76.

WE ARE EQUALLY IN NEED OF JESUS

It doesn't matter who we are—Jesus accepts us.

A quick glance around church on Sundays serves as a great reminder that rarely does one find so many different people gathered together for one common purpose. Individuals who normally would never venture outside their own social circle now extend their hands toward a stranger during the sign of peace. Despite all our many differences, the Church holds us together with miraculous unity. The divisions of society crumble within the love of God.

Truly in Christ there is neither male nor female, Gentile nor Jew, slave nor free person (Galatians 3:28). As the body of Christ, we need one another, and what separates us in the eyes of the world matters little in the embrace of Jesus. We are all equal at the Eucharist, for we are all fed from the same Lord and are all gathered at one table. We are nourished together but uniquely accepted, for each of us is given gifts and talents to build up the body, both individually and collectively. The Eucharist blesses us all in order that we might bless one another.

Whatever our worldly status, we are all equally in need of Jesus. As a child, I remember watching the movie *Rudolph the Red-Nosed Reindeer* and longing for the forgotten and broken gifts trapped on the Island of Misfit Toys to be rescued from their lonely existence. Surely there were children who would love them! In a way, we are all like those misfit toys, often considered broken and unimportant by the world and easily disposable.

Maybe at an earlier time in our lives, we were considered of value, a precious commodity to society, but now with our blemishes and oddities, our failures and average tendencies, we are no longer the up-and-coming but rather the down-and-out. Jesus takes us all: missing pieces, dirtied lives, and broken dreams, and gives us talents to invest. He gathers each of us in his salvific reach, knowing that we have been battered and abused by the world. Christ is our Good Samaritan, and he has room for each of us with him.

What I am and what I have are of value because of my acceptance by Christ. He loves me when others haven't. He knows me when many simply don't care. Jesus comes to the island of my loneliness and invites me to share in an authentic relationship with him. This enables me to truly "see" the people standing next to me, both in church and out, and accept them as Christ accepts me. I can live in fellowship, not only with those in my church who are so different from me, but also with those I encounter in my daily life. Today I hope to find Jesus in each person I meet.

Prayer Starter: How have I felt accepted by Christ? To whom can I reach out with a spirit of acceptance?

Rest in His Heart

True stability and contentment are found in Jesus.

The Annunciation is an amazing event within salvation history because the angel's message of hope is given to such an unlikely candidate: a young girl. Mary appears to be a small and unimportant person, certainly insignificant at first glance, and to the world clearly a minor player. But Mary's assent to God's will changes the world. God's standard is truly different from the world's!

We have a glimpse of this divine standard in the Old Testament when the prophet Samuel is told to go and select a new king for the children of God (1 Samuel 16:1-13). Samuel looks at Eliab and assumes that this is the man capable of ruling Israel, but God declares, "The LORD sees not as man sees; man looks on the outward appearance, but the LORD looks on the heart" (16:7).

The world didn't see the heart of Mary or David, and often the world doesn't see ours! The irony is that many of us spend our time trying to appear great in the eyes of others. We will go to such strenuous lengths for approval, even sacrificing what we know to be true for a temporal nod of affirmation from the powers that be.

Jesus comes to each of us in the Eucharist, and in many ways, it is our opportunity to rest in him. Jesus invites us to vulnerability. We can finally relax and let ourselves be loved.

The majority of us gathering for the Eucharist are not trying to impress Jesus with false piety or fancy clothes. We may try to do that for the other parishioners, but I think we realize that when we come to Jesus at Mass, we can, maybe for the first time all week, be ourselves. In the Eucharist, we can finally be accepted and satisfied.

Spending all of our energy on the whims of our world or the latest fancy of our culture will only lead us to loss and disquiet. Amidst the clamor, a word is given to us, and we have the opportunity to be like Mary, saying yes to what seems such an improbability: that God would want to be with us.

Jesus faithfully calls us to an authentic stability, a true encounter that is the fullness of that for which we are most longing. Jesus gives us himself, and because of this, our hearts find rest.

It is worth reflecting upon the idea that our hearts, resting in Christ, somehow remind Jesus of his mother's Immaculate Heart. Jesus never expects us to jump through societal hoops in order to gain his acceptance. He listens to our hearts, hears our cries and pains, feels our loss and aches, and in response he unites his Sacred Heart to our broken hearts. Why would he do this? Why does he care? Because Jesus is love. Love sees the internal heart, not the external show. Love freely chooses. Love sees possibilities and potentialities where the world sees limitations and failures.

In the end, does your heart beat for God? If so, you can know that his is already beating for you. We have seen what happened when Mary's heart beat for God—Jesus' heart was formed within her very body. What beauty will the world experience when our yes begins to be modeled on hers? What will happen when our two hearts, Jesus' Sacred Heart and our own wounded heart, unite?

Prayer Starter: In what ways can I truly experience rest in Jesus when I encounter him in the Eucharist? How can my heart be more like Mary's?

ENCOUNTERING JESUS IN ADORATION

Meeting Jesus in adoration is a gift,
a chance to show our love.

I frequently attend the Steubenville youth conferences, during which teens gather from around the country for prayer, praise, and fellowship. These conferences offer teachings, the sacraments, and opportunities to meet enthusiastic young Catholics from other cities and states. While I usually come to these events as a speaker or musical entertainer, I often leave renewed and refreshed in my own faith.

Over the years something has been happening in me at these conferences. Instead of being touched by a rich insight given in a homily or keynote address, I have found that my heart is moved as I see others encountering Jesus in profound ways, especially during adoration.

For many years now, adoration has been taking place on Friday and Saturday nights at the Steubenville conferences. This is the time when we encounter Jesus in the Eucharist. The consecrated Host is placed within a monstrance (from the Latin word *monstrare*, which means "to show") and displayed upon the altar for all to spend time with in prayer.

On Saturday, adoration is accompanied with a procession, with incense, candles, and bells ringing to let everyone know that our God is walking among us. In the room a spotlight follows the monstrance as the priest carries the Eucharist through the aisles. The first time I saw this many years ago, I was reminded of that Scripture verse from Philippians: "That at the name of Jesus every knee should bow, in heaven and on earth and under the earth, and every tongue confess that Jesus Christ is Lord, to the glory of God the Father" (Philippians 2:10-11). It is an amazing gift to witness Jesus passing in front of young men and women. You can truly see humanity responding with profound humility and sorrow at the realization of who is before them.

When you gather twenty-five hundred teens together and give them a chance to experience Jesus in such a visible way, things can get a little messy. Think of when Jesus was walking through the crowds. People weren't just silent as he went by. There were men and women calling out for healing and mercy and even in mockery as Jesus hung upon the cross (Luke 23:36). Our Lord truly evokes in us a need to respond. During one evening, a number of kids bravely yelled out, "I love you, Jesus!" It's as if they wanted to stare fear in the face and defy it by exposing their love for Christ as loudly as they could.

We adore Jesus who has come to us in such a humble way. We have a chance to respond to God with our bodies, bending our knees and raising our hands in appreciation. We are, after all, Eucharistic people, filled with thanksgiving!

Prayer Starter: How do I respond to Jesus in adoration?

DON'T GO WITHOUT

The Eucharist is the feast that nourishes us.

Have you ever had a long-distance relationship or had to spend days, weeks, or months apart from the one you loved? I can tell you from experience that it is no fun for either party. When you are captivated by love, the last thing you want is to be separated from your lover.

Our relationship with Christ is a relationship of love. But it isn't simply like the love we have for a spouse, a friend, or a child—it's all of these and much more. The love God has for us, this *agape* reality, is transformative, renewing, and life-giving. It causes a tangible reaction in us; it's like the reaction of someone who is seeing or hearing for the first time or tasting steak when they've only had dried bits of beef jerky. As Jesus says, it is like discovering a pearl of great price, something for which we are willing to sell all of our possessions to acquire (Matthew 13:46).

We were created to receive this type of love and, in doing so, become more authentic in our humanity than we could have previously imagined. Love from God is so indescribable because of his limitless and inexhaustible reality. We could say that receiving it is like attempting to funnel Niagara Falls into a straw. Realistically, it would destroy the straw, but in the true exchange, God enables us, the recipients, to receive this powerful love in a manner that we are capable of processing. The Eucharist is the overflow of actual love, truly, personally, entirely. Jesus is intentionally concealed in the bread and wine so that we have the opportunity to receive him. He is the entirety of what we long for and the provision and conduit that assist us in making a truly authentic response. It is this exchange of his heart with ours that creates the longing.

This encounter with God is beyond complete articulation, but he has revealed himself to us intentionally throughout time, showing us that even the limitations of creation will not hinder his generous reaching for us. God doesn't want us to be away from him for even a moment, so the constant opportunity to receive him in prayer and the sacraments fosters love every moment. God has gone out of his way so that we can hear, see, taste, and experience him. He now invites us to bring him to those who don't know what they are missing.

One of my close friends was at a Marian site where he unfortunately brought little money. He worried that he wouldn't have enough to buy something for his special someone at home if he used his funds for food every day, so he bought one loaf of bread to last him the five days. Every day he grabbed a chunk of bread and walked around the city, visiting the sites, praying, and learning about his faith. He would come home exhausted and hungry. On the last day of wandering about, he stumbled into the home in which he'd been residing, only to be greeted by the family who lived there. They said, "We've been wondering how you were doing. It seemed you were always on the go. We had a meal prepared for you every morning and night, but unfortunately, we missed you." He could have feasted every day! The meals were part of the cost of his lodging, and he went without basic nourishment when he never had to.

This is like our relationship with God. We often go without, starving because we can't afford more. God has paid for the feast and always wants us to participate in it with him. He always sets a place for us in the hope that we will receive his generosity. Truly we go without because we are really unaware of what it means to be loved by him. The Eucharist is the feast that nourishes us as we walk about and encounter the world. The Eucharist is the beautiful fulfillment of finally being reunited with our love.

Don't go without. God is ready to bless you with a beautiful reunification.

Prayer Starter: How often do I "go without"? Am I really taking advantage of the love that God offers me in prayer and the Eucharist?

I Got Jesus!

Our demeanor should witness to the importance
of our relationship with Jesus.

A year or two ago, I was on the road for a ministry event when I received a phone call from my wife. She told me that our son Jude had just received his First Communion. "What do you mean, he received his First Communion?" I asked. Jude hadn't even had his first confession, and the actual date for his First Communion was still a few years away.

Linda explained. Jude had gotten into line behind her at Mass to receive the Eucharist. Imitating everyone else, he held out his hands accordingly. Apparently, the priest didn't realize that little Jude hadn't received yet. Jude consumed our Lord and then walked back to his seat with a gigantic smile on his face. Snuggling next his mother and beaming with pride, he said, "I got me one of those!" Linda chuckled and realized that this was a very important moment and told Jude that he needed to spend some time praying for such a special gift. He was so well behaved after that!

I wish we all could be a little more like Jude that day. We often seem to take our Lord for granted. For a long time, Jude had wanted to receive the Eucharist. We kept telling him, "Soon, but not yet." His longing may not have been entirely pure, but I do think that it was more than just wanting to imitate his siblings. The joy of receiving Christ that day was visible in the way Jude smiled and behaved!

We are so very blessed by the availability of our Lord in the Eucharist. What an opportunity we've been given! The joy of the Lord is our strength (Nehemiah 8:10). Little Jude was filled with great joy that day. Our time with Jesus should really be visible in our demeanor, just as it was with Jude.

Have you ever met someone who is in love? There is no mistaking the signs. It can be a bit overwhelming! All they want to do is talk about their significant other, as if we really want to hear each and every nuance and detail. You can tell just by the look on their faces if they are having a good or bad day in their relationship.

We might need to be reminded that the One we receive every Sunday is the One who chose us to be in a relationship with him. While I don't get emotional every time I speak about my wife, I certainly do talk about her and my children at every event I am a part of. Why? Because they are my family. Linda is my love; this is my life! If you look at my Facebook or Twitter pages, you will see tons of pictures and comments about my family. I am still in love with my wife, and it really isn't a secret. I think that this is important when we talk about our relationship with the Eucharist. He "got" us and we "got" him. That is worth talking about!

Prayer Starter: Could someone tell by my demeanor that I am in love with Jesus?

Let Jesus Love You

God wants to lavish blessings upon you in the Eucharist. Let him!

One of the greatest lessons we can learn on earth is the truth that Jesus really does love us. We teach our children songs about his love, and, in fact, one of the best-known attributes about God is that he is love! We have the verbiage down fairly well, but I'm not sure how much we have the truth of it in our hearts.

I have a friend who is an alcoholic. I have talked with her on good days and bad days, and the bad days can be pretty rough. One day I could tell that she was frustrated at having to tell me the same story, a story of failure. In no uncertain terms, I told her that even if she told me every week that she had failed, I would still love her. I insisted that my family and I would always welcome her, that we unequivocally accepted her. She has been sober for almost a year, and I couldn't be more proud of her. But if she called and said it went badly the previous night, I would tell her the same thing: we love you—greatly and unconditionally.

That's what I'm talking about! That's what we rarely see. That, my friends, is what we need and what the world is waiting for. Will we love people even if they don't change? While we are all called to be saints, that doesn't mean that we turn up our noses at those who are struggling with sins that are seemingly so far beneath us now. From personal experience, let me tell you that it is far easier to sin and get back into old habits than it is to stay constant, and the surest way to slip and fall is to embrace pride.

Being a saint is not a matter of how little we fail or stumble in our spiritual walk; rather, it is a matter of how much we let Jesus love us in our brokenness and weaknesses. The great example in the Scriptures is the Father in the parable of the prodigal son (Luke 15:11-32). The father unconditionally loves his son even after he has offended his family, himself, and his religion. The forgiveness that is offered is so beyond our rational understanding that almost anyone who hears it recognizes a demonstration of love that is otherworldly.

The father in the story also goes out to the older brother, who is frustrated and angry that the fattened calf is being sacrificed. Many people relate to the older son, especially if they have not wandered off like the younger son but have remained true to the Lord. Their lives may seem like less a reason for celebration. And yet the story shows us a father who goes out to both of his sons and invites them into a celebration, which is above and beyond what anyone would have expected. After all, this sacrifice is being held during a time of famine, and yet the father seemingly wastes the best, the future meals, for his sons. The word "prodigal" means "to lavish," and in this story, the father lavishes both of his sons with love.

The problem with both of these boys is that they don't realize who and whose they are. The younger son thinks he should return as a servant, and the older son thinks he is a slave. But they are both sons of a loving father who has never looked at them as employees but rather as his own flesh and blood. He loves them and has been waiting for a chance to help them see this without ambiguity.

This story speaks to our hearts, and we know that it is God who loves us so unconditionally. Remember the fattened calf in the story that is sacrificed? God gave us Jesus as the best sacrifice so that we might truly celebrate. The meal we receive in the Eucharist is a constant reminder that God has lavished everything upon us, the wayward child and the embittered and resentful one, so that we would come in and join in the celebratory meal. Whether you have come from a long distance or are just beginning to see things differently right where you are, God is ready to remind you that you are truly his, and you are truly home.

How do you know God forgives you? Look at the cross and see the complete and total generosity of love. How do you know that your sins are really forgiven? Look at the cross and see the invitation to come and participate in the meal. I wonder if one day the younger son questioned—maybe even for just a second—whether his father had really forgiven him. But if he had looked out at the empty pen, he would have realized that the fattened calf was gone!

See, Jesus doesn't regret his great and total gift on our behalf, because the love of the Trinity is so authentic, constant, and complete. We really may have a hard time understanding this love because it is very different from what we have experienced thus far. But if you let him, I think God will remind you that he is your Father and that he wants to lavish his love on you. Let him love you now. Don't wait!

Prayer Starter: Am I the wayward child or the embittered one? How has the lavish love of the Father changed my heart?

Part Two
Eucharistic Presence

What's He Doing Here?

We need to invite Jesus into our lives.

Many years ago I spent a day ministering at a parish in Pennsylvania. I gave numerous talks and performed some music, and overall, it was a busy and wonderful time. I had taken my family along with me, and as is often the case, the afternoon culminated in the final event, the celebration of Mass. Most of my children were still very young, and my son Kolbe happened to be sitting next to me. This church had a very large crucifix hanging from the ceiling, with metal chains holding the wooden crossbeam. Kolbe was quite transfixed by the crucifix, and at some point right at the beginning of Mass, he looked at me and said, "Jesus!"

Now I was a pretty proud poppa already, but seeing the amazing fruit of our parental theological formation on the mind and heart of Kolbe was proof positive that we had certainly gotten things right with this fifth child! (The crucifix was quite large, so looking back, the fact that he recognized Jesus was not as earth-shattering as I may have possibly imagined at the time.) Usually, when I do talks and have my family present, there is a lot of interest in my kids. In this case, I was certain people were amazed at the profound grasp of my child's Christology. I looked down at Kolbe and affirmed his statement. "Yes, Kolbe, that's Jesus."

My head got a little big during this time as I patted myself on the back, so to speak. Little Kolbe's recognition of our Lord was no small matter to me, and in a way it made sense. He had been attending Mass most of his life, and we had tons of rosaries and Mary statues all over the house. So I guessed that if any kids were going to "get it," it would be Kolbe.

At that moment, he looked up at me and asked, "What's he doing here?" Well, this was unexpected. I stumbled around for a moment and replied, "Well, he's in the tabernacle and he's in your heart." And Kolbe said, "How'd he get in here?" At that point, the woman sitting right behind us, who had hired me for the event and had witnessed my daylong catechesis to her parish, began to laugh quite visibly. So much for keeping up appearances!

I love telling this story because it highlights the beauty of our growing in the understanding of Jesus' presence in our lives. I have often thought that many adults are asking a similar question as they go about their lives: "What's he doing here?" Jesus really is present for us at all times, readily available for us to cling to in crisis, to join us in celebrations, and to assist us in times of difficulty. I don't know why we forget that Jesus truly longs to be present in our lives. I think at times people will have a moment in church when they suddenly realize, "Hey, wait a minute—I feel Jesus here with me, right now." To that I say, "Of course, and he's with us even when we don't feel him!" So how'd he get in here? The truth is that Jesus is always making a way to be with us.

It is easy to teach people about Jesus. I can read a lot of books and information about the Church and the Scriptures, even meditating on the life of Jesus over the centuries by reading the writings of the saints. But in the end, I am invited to know Jesus personally. St. John writes about a Jesus whom he knows so well, whom he has seen and heard (1 John 1:3), and, of course, upon whose breast he leaned against at the Last Supper (John 13:25). John is so close to Jesus that on the cross, Jesus gives Mary to him to bring to his very home (John 19:26-27). We need to foster this relationship and realize that Jesus is waiting for us to recognize him in our daily lives.

One other response to the question of "How'd he get in here?" could easily be "We have invited him here." We are often surprised that Jesus is present with us in our daily moments, but his presence does not necessarily mean that we go to him or seek him in our need. This has to be something that we truly and intentionally try to do: recognize that Jesus is there with us, and then welcome him into that moment. We are ultimately the ones who can invite Jesus to bring to fruition in us that which he has already begun in baptism. As we learn to do this—to invite Jesus into each of our moments—we can easily speak to others about the surprising presence of Christ in their own lives. They may find his presence astonishing in light of all of their offenses and distractions, and yet Jesus offers his salvific healing to each and every one of us.

As Kolbe grows older, I am sure there will be other moments in his life when he will be surprised to see Jesus' presence. He will have the choice to invite him into that moment and realize that the answer to "How'd he get in here?" is in reality entirely up to him.

Prayer Starter: When did I recently invite Jesus into the moments of my day? When may I have forgotten to do so?

RECEIVE

*Allow God to give you the gifts he
offers in the Eucharist.*

One day I had the chance to spend some time with my
dad before heading off to an event in Minnesota.
We had coffee and some lunch together, bundled
up against the weather, and visited a few bookstores, just
enjoying one another's company. He is always trying to give
me his sweaters and gloves, and often if I attempt to pay for
food or even a whimsical purchase, he beats me to it, insisting
that I put my money away for another time. That night at
dinner, we talked about our family, our careers, which brands
of beer we like, and whatever else came up. We don't have to
have an agenda about what we discuss, and we don't panic
if the conversation has a lull. In fact, there really aren't any
limitations or places we don't feel free to address. We talk
about the difficulties of the past, poor decisions, concerns
with money or health, and the future. This time was just
what I needed. Time spent with my dad is time well spent.

When I sit in church waiting for Mass to begin, I enjoy the
quiet of the sanctuary, and right before me is Jesus, present in
the Blessed Sacrament. I don't have to have an agenda when
I come into Jesus' presence. We sit and talk about things
that are happening in my life, and there are no areas that are
off-limits. Jesus has permission to ask me anything he wishes,

and he has given me permission to ask anything of him. I have been invited into the beauty of the family of God, and that means that he, on a much grander scale than my earthly father, wants to bless me and provide for me.

God cares about my whimsical purchases, my financial concerns, my physical needs, and my greatest longings. He has not left me on my own to figure out how to make everything work; rather, I am given the opportunity to receive.

This word "receive" is really at the heart of our relationship. From my earthly father, I have received physical life, financial assistance, idiosyncratic tendencies, and vocal similarities and expressions. In my walk with God as Father, I have received the opportunity to live in a way that is more authentic than I could have previously imagined. I really can live heroically, resting upon the heritage of the family and our propensity for greatness in Christ. I am treated with blessings and favor, knowing that the closer I come to love and imitate the Eucharist, the more I will look like and act like the man I am called to be.

It isn't always easy to let someone else provide for you, but the willingness to receive all that Jesus gives to us in the Eucharist provides us with the strength to become a gift to others. In other words, we must receive from the Lord in order to give back to those around us. This gift of ourselves to others around us is in some unique way an actual gift back to God in that he identifies himself with the small and weak, the thirsty and needy. We are not meant to be a storehouse as much as a conduit, having grace flowing in us in order that it might flow out from us to those around us.

Relationships are often difficult this side of eternity. In our families we don't regularly say the right things or do what needs to be done in a timely fashion or even forgive quickly when wronged. We often make a habit of picking at the festering wounds of those closest to us rather than being the healing balm that we should and could be. Jesus is inviting us, through our reception of the Eucharist, to truly begin to offer healing and forgiveness to those around us. We receive Christ in order to give Christ to those within our reach.

Just as it would be strange to look at my dad during an awkward silence and begin to read from a paper that listed phrases to use when the conversation lulled, so it would be in our time with Jesus. Our relationship with Christ is neither superficial nor artificial. He is waiting to speak the word to us that we really need to hear. He is willing to listen to everything that is cluttering our brains, and he is even ready to carry the weight of our concerns when we are ready to relinquish them.

I think my dad wants to bless me; he wants to be in my life and hear my stories, and he would love to offer any advice I'd be willing to take. God wants to bless you today; he wants to be in your life and desires to hear your stories. He would love to offer you advice on anything you would be willing to share with him. Why? Because he is truly our

Father, and he longs for us to receive the many gifts he continues to pour out upon us.

Prayer Starter: I will spend time talking to Jesus as I would to my closest friend. What gift might he want to give to me?

Priorities

Just being silently present with Jesus is enough.

Since my teenager, Noah, started playing football at school, we've enjoyed watching NFL games together. We don't feel the need to talk about anything important; rather, the time we spend together is the important thing. Tonight my love of Jesus is best demonstrated in letting Noah stay up a little later than his usual bedtime just to watch the game with his dad. We have this moment together, and it is a moment that is helping me to be a better father. I think it is also a moment in which my son realizes that he and I have something special going on.

I remember as a small boy watching the Steelers play the Cowboys with my best friends. Those were great memories. What would have made those moments even better is if I could have watched those games with my father, who was an exceptional athlete in his own right. Unfortunately, my father and mother were not able to reconcile their differences, and as a result, I spent a lot of time without my dad present. I loved being with my friends, and as far as friendships go, they were amazing, but I really loved being with my dad more.

I am a married man with many children, and the Jesus I will most often encounter on a regular basis is the Christ in them. Are there times for me to go and kneel before Jesus in the Eucharist? Of course! But tonight I sit in a big black chair with my teenage boy and watch a game that we both enjoy.

The two activities aren't opposed to each other. We don't either watch a game with our child or go to adoration: when we do the former, we are doing the latter as well. I apply this principle when I spend hours after school throwing the ball back and forth with my own kids along with half the neighborhood. I am not writing anything profound during that time of catch, yet I am being present to my children and others right where they are in life.

There is something profound about loving Christ in the person who is next to you. That is one of the main fruits of spending time with Jesus in the Blessed Sacrament. People all over the world are experiencing the joy of the presence of Christ in Eucharistic adoration, but it must become tangible once each person walks out into the real world.

In some small way, I am showing my son a picture of fatherly love just by being with him, and my hope is that when he starts to spend time in adoration, he will find it somewhat familiar, like being with his father. In no way am I comparable with God as a father, and yet I do hold that title with humble reverence. As my son simply sits in my presence, we don't have to say a word for us to remember this event. I can be with him and he can be with me; and that is good. In reality, when we sit with Jesus in adoration, it is such an exchange, we with him and he with us. We don't even have to say anything for it to be significant.

I am always amazed at Noah's appetite after he plays football. Whether his team wins or loses, he plays hard and has learned some great lessons about teamwork. The more I learn about my son, the more amazed and impressed I am. He is turning into a wonderful young man right before my eyes. As a father, it is an inexplicable joy to watch him grow.

I truly believe the Lord loves for us to be in his presence because he simply loves being with us, just as I love being with my son. There are a number of ways for us to contemplate this topic of presence, but sometimes I think it is more about silence than words spoken, about being in the same room and just knowing we are together.

Prayer Starter: How can I become more aware of Christ in my family members? How might that awareness change the way I relate to them?

STEADY AND CONSTANT

*Christ in the Eucharist has a constant presence
that is available to us at all times.*

The Spirit is always moving, always ready to fill us to overflowing, always present and comforting, always reminding and inviting! The difficulty is with us. We move away from him; we are content with the least; we are absent or inattentive; we forget his presence and can be disinterested when he calls us. The Spirit of God is a Person and will never force us to walk with him (Galatians 5:16). It is our choice!

This idea of constancy is not one that we fully comprehend. How can anyone be entirely anything? We are used to the fickle, the temporal, the inconsistent, and the average. Why we are ready to be average is probably understandable, but it is not our purpose. And we do have examples of what consistent faithfulness can look like. The steady and steadfast bond of a mother and a father united in holy matrimony and choosing to love one another, even when each of their flaws is readily visible, points to a God who cannot be detoured from loving his creation and reflects that truth for the couple themselves, for their children, and even for the world. Of course, we could probably see the converse—a couple inclined to conditional commitment ultimately reassures the world that no such steadfast love exists.

The steady and constant love of Jesus for us is not just seen in the primordial pillar of holy matrimony; it is also truly demonstrated in the Eucharistic presence of the Lord in the tabernacles throughout the world. Think of it like this: the same Jesus we encounter in the Blessed Sacrament today is the One whom St. Francis knelt before and received at Mass. This constant Christ is the One St. Ignatius of Loyola wished to follow with knightly faithfulness. Our precious Little Flower was captivated with the very Jesus that you can visit at any moment in the Eucharist. We would do well to remember that Jesus looks at us—always—ready to reassure and affirm that our lives are not only beautiful but are meant to truly have an impact in the world.

While we certainly do enjoy the change that happens with new fashions and technological advancements, I think there is something about the human condition that recognizes the need for a bulwark amidst the storms of life. We enjoy visiting new places, but we need an anchor to hold us firm and in one place. Following Jesus is really the adventure we've all longed for. While no saint's story is the same, there is always within that story the same solidity and constancy of Christ's love. It is a love unaffected even today by the attention-deficit disorder of our culture. The more we cling to Jesus as our rock and shield, our strong tower, our victory and eternal advocate, the more confident we will be when we face all that is unsteady. We surely need this grounding in Christ, and believing him to be that rock will foster our advancement in holiness.

Thanks be to God that he has seen people like you and me over the years and is neither surprised nor baffled about what to do with lives such as ours. Jesus waits for us to take comfort in his faithfulness, ensuring our steady walk with him. He will always want to be with us; he will always want our sanctity and our small successes, even our failures. Jesus will always and forever await our feeble efforts and our insignificant contributions; he is always inclined to reassure our fluttering and worried heart. Why? Because he is Love, and love keeps no record of wrong. Love believes all things, hopes all things, and, in fact, never ends (1 Corinthians 13:4-8). We need this type of solid relationship in our lives, not just occasionally, but always!

Prayer Starter: How is Jesus in the Eucharist the one constant in my life amid the changes I face?

Jesus, Present in Our Storms

Jesus understands our trials and is there for us.

I am so sick, and so is my family! High temperatures, ER visits, medications—this is obviously an event that was not on our to-do list. And with nine kids, inevitably all will eventually come down with some variation of this viral theme.

There are two things I want to talk about in this reflection. First, Jesus is able to be present with us in our storms. Not hypothetically present or just as an ethereal nod that God is in control; Jesus is actually and truly able to be present for us in a redemptive way whenever we go through the storms in life. He cares when we are sick, when our children are ill, and when we feel as if we can't go on. Jesus is really there for us when we don't have all the answers as to why suffering takes place.

Remember that passage in which Jesus is walking on water (Matthew 14:22-33)? Matthew articulates an important truth in this account of Jesus. The disciples are told to get into the boat and head to the other side of the water, but as they journey, the wind and waves overtake them in a storm, and all of their attention is consumed with remaining afloat. It is in this moment of crisis that Jesus simply walks to them on the water. This is a great example of grace building on nature: Jesus chooses the natural reality of a storm to demonstrate his power over the natural elements. But an even greater demonstration of his limitlessness is as a divine Person. He tells the men in the boat, "It is I; have no fear" (14:27). I simply love Peter's response: "Lord, if it is you, bid me come to you on the water" (14:28).

I think you and I would have said, "Lord, if it's you, get in the boat, calm the storm, and quit freaking us out!" But after hearing Jesus say, "Come," Peter steps out on the water. The storm remains as Peter walks, but the distractions of the storm cause him to take his eyes off of Christ, and he sinks. Jesus is so patient with all of us. The wandering eyes are fixed back upon Christ, Peter is saved, and those in the boat declare and affirm that Jesus is truly the Son of God. The point for us is that Jesus knows our physical and spiritual distractions, our illnesses, our worries, and our storms in life, and he wants us to know that he is present. Jesus' presence comes to us often in a way that is different from what we are used to. He is not limited by natural restrictions. We can hope in Christ that our storms are not going to consume us.

The second point I want to make is this: Jesus is a real Person. He is fully man and like us in all things except sin. I am fond of saying this because I find that often, even in our approach to the Eucharist, our minds and eyes start to wander all over the place. We think of Jesus as if he were a mist that we shortly expect to appear instead of being actually there before us, hidden behind the "accidents" of bread and wine.

I'm not sure why we are afraid to acknowledge Jesus' humanity. Even the early Church struggled with a heresy that looked upon the flesh as evil. The Gnostics wanted a way out of this messy humanity, and with a secret insight and a select group, they could easily look down upon all of the fleshly distractions. The problem with this line of thought is that in the Incarnation, the Second Person of the Blessed Trinity became flesh and dwells among us (John 1:14). God chose to become man! This act radically changes our perspective of what it means to be a human person. Jesus as the New Adam sets aright that which had been overturned by the first Adam's disobedience.

So when we look at our lives with all of its feverish moments, sniffles, and visits to the doctors, it isn't as if we approach a God who has no understanding of the human condition. Jesus truly comes and comforts the battered body, for he knows its limitations. While we might find ourselves stressed or frustrated with circumstances beyond our control, Jesus reminds us that God cares for us even more than the sparrows or the beautiful flowers adorned with God's creative handiwork (Matthew 6:28; 10:29-30). Jesus doesn't despise or look down upon our humanity because he fully is a man! While Jesus is one Person with two natures (human and divine), we, of course, are one person with one nature. His humanity and divinity in one Person (called the "hypostatic union") should blow our minds, to be sure, but it doesn't change the truth that Jesus is fully a man who knows what it is like to be lied to, betrayed, denied, hurt, and misunderstood.

What we have the chance to do is offer all of our frustrations, illnesses, and seemingly impossible scenarios to Jesus as a gift, which in a truly miraculous way can become redemptive. In other words, Jesus has made it possible for us to join in his salvific work at the cross by uniting all our struggles and losses with his entire gift of self back to the Father in the love of the Holy Spirit, which then can become graces poured out on those needing a miracle.

What I think is important here is to recognize that the storms do come, but Jesus, personally knowing our human condition, gives us a chance to do something with the storm: we can stand amid the mayhem and witness to the glory of God at work. This will affect not only you. Just as the disciples in the boat cried out in acknowledging God's presence among them, so too will you become a witness of God's work to others around you who see you remaining afloat amidst great difficulties.

Prayer Starter: Where was Jesus in my last storm? Did I recognize his presence?

Part Three:
Strength for the Journey

Run to the Eucharist!

Don't forget that you are in a battle!

It doesn't have to be a big thing that causes us to feel out of sorts. We could be having a good day when suddenly a negative comment is made that sinks deeply into our hearts. Every ounce of joy flutters away. There are also days when we wake up and feel as if everything is off center, and we're not even sure why we feel so glum. Without a plan, we can easily find ourselves blindsided by circumstances and tossed about by every emotional whim.

First, I would remind you of a basic truth: you are in a battle. The enemy has a great desire to keep you distracted from your heavenly goal. If you are focused inward, then you will certainly not see those in need around you. You need to be alert and aware that our foe plays dirty and will try to steal or destroy your intimacy with Christ! If you are not careful, the impact of this diabolical blindsiding can take you out of the game for a time.

Second, you are not in this alone! Quit trying to do everything! You don't have to field every opposing remark, address every emotional disturbance, or discover every missing insight all on your own. Jesus is there, ready to fight for you! Jesus will enable you to gain strength because he cares for you, even more than the sparrows and lilies of the fields. You have the family of God at your disposal to assist you in your daily battles. In an odd way, this news may be somewhat of a surprise when the rubber meets the road. What I mean is that in an otherwise impossible situation, you may find Christ present, and this loving stability enables you to deal with a crisis or a scenario in a way you couldn't previously imagine. If we begin to rest and let him take over, we will find that our defense is far sturdier than we might have thought.

And finally, when we feel out of sorts, we would do well to remember that Jesus has not left us orphans (John 14:18). We have his very Spirit in us, and this, my friends, is not insignificant. With Jesus giving himself to us in the Eucharist, the collaborative work of the saints on our behalf, and the Holy Spirit breathing new life into us, our victory is guaranteed. In fact, we are more than conquerors through Christ who loved us (Romans 8:37). The burden that you are carrying is too much for you to carry or battle on your own. Let Jesus be the rest you need today.

Remember too that while you may not be able to go to Mass daily or get to adoration regularly, Jesus is still there for you, encouraging you to ask for his assistance. Not only will he help you in your personal difficulties, but he has also provided you with an army of saints to intercede for you. At times, certain saints will seem closer to you than before, and this is the Lord's way of letting you know who is advocating for you in your time of difficulty.

Maybe we have forgotten that Jesus is present in our exhaustion. Possibly we consider our difficulties to be too insignificant for the Lord's time and attention, but the truth is quite the opposite. Every weary moment, along with each distracting thought and difficult day, is of great interest and concern to our Savior. Jesus wants you to walk in the victory that he has provided through his salvific work. Jesus will certainly not force you to rest in him or bully you to share your burdens with him, but his invitation stands nonetheless. Place your weary heart and aching soul into the healer's hands!

Jesus gives himself to us in the Eucharist, not only so that we can be nourished, but also so that we can remember that we are not alone on this pilgrimage. Jesus is true compassion that is extended to us in our daily grind. Yes, the enemy won't give up trying to distract us or attempting to lead us by every emotional whim and fancy. But Christ Jesus knows his lies and knows most effectively how to assist us in leaving them behind. We just need to willingly give our burdens and pain to Jesus. As he says, "Come to me, all who labor and are heavy laden, and I will give you rest" (Matthew 11:28).

Today you should remember just how much you've been loved. Not only are your sins forgiven through Jesus' saving act upon the cross, but you are also assisted in your journey into eternity. Run to the Eucharist. Gather strength against the bombardments of the enemy, and realize that you only need to place these cares into the loving hands of Jesus. Rest, my friends, because you are greatly loved! If we realize this truth during our difficult days, I believe something amazing can happen: we can blindside hell with holy love! Our greatest victory over being blindsided is allowing Christ to become more and more involved in our difficult days.

Prayer Starter: How can I allow Christ to be more involved in my difficult days or when I feel distracted or tempted by the enemy?

Ground to Stand On

The Eucharist is the truth we can cling to.

Indifference, sarcasm, skepticism, and compromise—these can all quietly and subtly creep into our behavior. So in order for us to stand up against the beginnings of what, years from now, we might otherwise look upon with regret, we need to ask ourselves these questions: "Where are the lines blurred in my life and beliefs? In what ways am I leaving myself open to evil?"

Thankfully we have the Eucharist, which gives us true ground to stand on amidst the advancement of the world and its ever-changing standards. The Eucharist gives to us an authentic voice of intentionality within a world of selective indifference or biting sarcasm and skepticism. It is the Eucharist that keeps the lines from blurring because Jesus is truth. He is not *like* truth; rather, Jesus *is* truth. Any truth that we might echo, affirm, recognize, or even hold onto is just a tiny bit of the entirety that Jesus is.

I don't believe we are to live in fear, but we would do well to remember the story of the virgins who were encouraged to keep oil in their lamps and their wicks trimmed because at any moment, the groom would arrive (Matthew 25:1-13). The Eucharist helps us to keep a heavenly perspective when the world demands that we see things selfishly. The Eucharist enables us to modify our desires with the virtue of temperance when everyone around us seems to be finding new ways to gratify every possible passion. The Eucharist stands in direct opposition to the devil and his lies because the truth will not bend before darkness. The Eucharist steadies our hearts when they skip with worry and secures our ground when the storms increase, because Jesus is ever present and ever true. It may seem like a long time ago, but the Eucharist was of such importance in the early Church that young St. Tarcisius sacrificed his life trying to bring our Lord to those Christians condemned to death.

We applaud our sports teams for each inch gained in the games that are played, and we recognize as heroic that soldier who runs into the enemy territory to rescue a fallen peer. The world will want to consume us and take the ground that we stand upon, but we must fight with a holy tenacity. We must rescue our fallen friends and family, even if it means that we advance into enemy territory so that we might carry them back home to safety.

What does this look like? It might be your prayers today before the Eucharist that give solid footing to your fallen-away family member. It is possible that your prayer during Mass may be the grace that pours into the battle that your friend is fighting, granting them victory when they normally would fall to ruin. We are in a battle, and in Christ we truly have the victory. Let's give that solid victory as a gift to as many people as we can today! Hold steady, my friends—we have something worth fighting for and holding onto. We have truth, we have light, and we have the Eucharist!

Prayer Starter: What areas of my life need strengthening in the Eucharist?

BE NEEDY

We need him, so let's not be afraid to admit it.

The other day I sent this note to my friend: "I pray you will realize how messy you are today so that you will remember that you still need Jesus. Be needy for Christ!"

I have been soaking in that word, recognizing its importance for others and for me. For most of us, it can be very difficult to acknowledge our need to others. It certainly is difficult to let down our guard and allow people to see that we really don't have it all together.

We certainly don't encourage needy behavior in others. As a society, we don't want people to be on long-term assistance, and we complain when we think that those receiving it aren't working hard enough to become independent. We also discourage needy behaviors on a psychological level. People who are codependent may be a burden on others and often need clinical treatment just to survive. The fact is that we don't seem to have a lot of tolerance for needy people. It is easy to look down our noses on those who haven't been given our specific gifts and talents or financial opportunities.

What we need here is humility. We need to recognize the spiritual and emotional neediness that is part of our human condition. We all have an intrinsic need for relationships. I need to be heard, to be understood, to be valued and appreciated, and ultimately, I need to be loved. The truth of our condition is apparent: there isn't a single person who can meet all of our needs. Only Christ will.

But although we might all agree that our ultimate fulfillment lies in Christ, how does this affirmation of truth make it into our day-to-day lives? Our actions solidify our beliefs, and our beliefs motivate our actions. If we reason that Jesus is the answer, then we must act upon this truth. By walking into church and kneeling before Jesus in the Eucharist, even for a only few minutes when the occasion presents itself, we are declaring with our bodies that we still need Jesus. When we make the Sign of the Cross as we drive by a church, we participate in the belief that the Eucharist is worthy of adoration, and our response is fitting, since we still have need of him. We cannot halfheartedly mumble that Jesus might be the one who can meet our needs and expect that the emotions we experience will feel centered in the love of God.

Knowing that we have a need doesn't necessarily mean we are failures. Instead, acknowledging our need for Christ simply ensures that we will run to him. If I pretend I am not terribly sick, insisting that my body is a bulwark of strength and health, over time I will die from lack of medical attention. If, on the other hand, I recognize that an illness I am experiencing can be deadly if left unattended, then I will be able to quickly address the problem with a solution.

Pretending that we have somehow reached spiritual maturation is a springboard into sin and self-implosion. Why?

Because that is the definition of pride—an ungrounded self-confidence. If Christ is healing me, my confidence is limitless. When my need is being filled with the Spirit of Christ, this not only ensures my ultimate healing but also fosters a grounded confidence. When we come to Jesus in prayer, visit our Eucharistic Lord, or receive him at Mass, it is a constant reminder and a statement of truth that we still need Jesus' real presence in our lives. We are not hypochondriacs; rather, we are people regularly awaiting the healing presence of Christ to address our real needs. We will always need Jesus!

When we recognize our needs, we have two choices. We can run to the solutions that the world offers us in an attempt to entertain or numb ourselves from it all. This will never satisfy us. Alternatively, we can give our needs to Jesus. He will never reject us; rather, he is waiting with expectation to give us the healing that we most need.

Let Jesus satisfy your need today. Don't just mouth the words, but do something about it. He emphatically invites us to come to him, all of us who are weak and heavy laden, so that we can know his love. Jesus is never afraid or surprised by our need. Let Jesus love you. After all, you really do need him!

Prayer Starter: How can I demonstrate my need for Jesus today?

Part Four:
Repentance and Forgiveness

Jesus, I'm Sorry!

God invites us to be honest about our sin.

We were nearing the end of an evening of Eucharistic adoration at a youth conference of twenty-five hundred teens. After the procession, the monstrance containing the Host was placed back upon the altar. Suddenly I heard a boy to my right cry out, "I'm sorry, Jesus." Even writing this now, I am moved to tears, as I was on that night. This young man echoed, I believe, the heart of us all: true sorrow for our sins.

While we often want to cry out our love for Christ, it is a more difficult thing to acknowledge so publicly our need for forgiveness. I don't know that I heard a truer statement from anyone that weekend. Another member on the speaking team was weeping beside me. This boy's cry of sorrow touched us all so deeply. He proclaimed something that we all need to say: "Jesus, I'm so sorry."

Admitting our guilt is not easy. We like our sins to remain in darkness. We often hope that no one will really see how broken we are; in fact, we are certain that everyone would flee if they encountered the real us. But Jesus walks among us in the Eucharist, and he sees our true self. He notices everything we are and everything we are not.

Remember the words of St. Paul to the Romans? While we were yet sinners, Christ died for us (5:8). If Jesus had such love for us while we were sinners, how much more will he not abandon us after we have come to him? In other words, yes, you will stumble and fall. You will erect false ideas about yourself and hide behind walls and masks. You will forget what you've learned and have to relearn it again. But God sees your true self, your hidden mess, and never forgets his love for you!

I will never know that boy's story, but I do know that his confession and his need for Jesus touched me. I want to be like that. I want to cry out on a daily basis that I am a sinner in need of my Savior. St. John reminds us that confession of our sins brings about forgiveness and cleansing (1 John 1:9). As Jesus comes to you today—and he will, even if you are not kneeling before the Eucharist in adoration—how will you respond?

In the event that you feel the desire to be vulnerable to Jesus and to invite him into the dark places of your life, I promise you this: the light of his love will enable you to be the saint that God has called you to be. Sorrow for sin brings us healing and purity. Sorrow for sin brings us to the realization that the world can't satisfy us. Christ sees our sorrow and does not leave us in our brokenness. Like the Good Samaritan, he comes before us in order to heal and nurture us (Luke 10:25-37).

Thanks be to God for the opportunity to be honest about where we are and where we want to be! The surest way to grow in our relationship with Jesus is to walk in honest vulnerability. Going to Confession always gives us the perfect act of contrition that we need, even if our feelings don't accompany it. Confession is necessary for us to grow with Christ. But you don't have to wait for Confession to tell Jesus you are sorry. You can do an examination of conscience every night and tell him everything. And you may as well be honest, since he already knows where you have fallen short.

Jesus is ready to love you right now! Who knows, maybe your sorrow for your sin will touch someone you don't even know. I have come to realize that when you and I think about the true presence of Jesus in the Eucharist—when we attend Mass or spend time in adoration—we often become acutely aware of our need for him. While many are afraid of the light of Jesus pouring into the hidden places of our lives, the truth is, that light enables us to be sorry. Being repentant is not an end in itself, however. Jesus wants to confront us so that we can be healed, so that we can be forgiven. That's the best part!

Jesus invites us to see him, to be honest about our sin, and to be healed and forgiven. The end of sorrow for sin is celebration with him!

Prayer Starter: Am I ready to tell Jesus that I'm sorry? What do I need to confess and be forgiven of?

BE VULNERABLE

Don't be afraid to let your guard down with Jesus.

Sometimes we are afraid of being vulnerable with others. We fear sharing our true self, and so we cling to a false representation of who we really are. We wear masks in the presence of strangers, hoping that this will somehow endear ourselves to them. Not only do we often build up an idealized representation of ourselves for each of our social interactions, but we also erect walls to protect ourselves so that we can't be hurt. The irony is that those we meet are likely offering us a false version of themselves. So we rarely have true interactions or brush up against the true person hidden behind that false representation.

Why do we fear being vulnerable and allowing others to see us in our weakness? Here is the reality: we are all a mess! And knowing how much God has met our needs should free us to accept others in their mess.

If I am truly in need and I run to the open arms of the *Abba* Father whom Jesus has revealed to me, then I find myself loved, possibly for the first time. Jesus' love is extended to me while I am yet a sinner. He holds nothing back, as demonstrated by his total self-sacrifice upon the cross. Even my best day will still be eternally unworthy of love from a self-existing, eternal Being who is beyond my greatest ability to even describe. If God can love me so entirely in my greatest sin, then how much more will I not be rejected when I flounder about after being baptized into his very life?

As we continually reflect on this truth, we are free to love someone who is even "messier" than we are. Christ loves them as well, and knowing that I am constantly in need of Jesus allows me the clarity to see how entirely my Father loves this person before me.

I remember going to Confession to a priest who was somewhat moved by a talk I'd given the previous year. After going to the Sacrament of Reconciliation, the priest said to me, "So you're just like us." But the truth is that we are all needy, and therefore we have nothing to boast of except the cross of Christ (Galatians 6:14). That is what St. Paul said, and he also called himself the "foremost of sinners" (1 Timothy 1:15). I have nothing to offer another person except this truth: I am really loved by God! And do you know what? So are you! We are all sinners and still in need of our Savior! That, my friends, is truly good news! This is *the* good news!

The saints, who established a pattern of saying yes to God's will, still found themselves flawed and broken. It is the grounding of our authentic life in the salvific work of Jesus that causes the strength and consistency of Christ to become revealed through our weakness. My constant confession of authentically needing Jesus gives me the freedom to love others. I am free to go out and live in a radical way, to fully love those who are the outcasts in the world.

Jesus had within his closest group men longing for favored positions of authority, men who became angry, misunderstood his mission, and betrayed and denied him. Jesus still loved them, and he still loves us. Sometimes I think that people look at the Church and say, "Well, I'm too weak and sinful to be a part of that." But if we are vulnerable with others, then we become witnesses that Jesus still accepts broken and messy people. Thank God!

Prayer Starter: Does my awareness of my constant need of Jesus allow me to freely love others in spite of their inadequacies? Do I allow myself to be vulnerable with others?

COURAGEOUS ANALYSIS

*Let Jesus shine a light on the dark places
so that he can heal you.*

The Trappist monk Thomas Merton once observed, "Our ability to see ourselves objectively and to criticize our own actions, our own failings, is the source of a very real strength."[2] However, most of us do not generally find ourselves inclined to give an honest assessment of our failings. After all, ignorance is bliss. If we can avoid the reality of our flaws, then we can continue in a "business as usual" mode.

But Jesus wants more than just business as usual for us. Have you ever wondered why God placed within human persons a gauge that helps us to determine whether what we are about to do is right or wrong? Or, put another way, have you ever wondered why certain things seem as if they ought not be done, while others seem as if they ought to be done? The reason is that God has given each of us a conscience. With an honest sobriety concerning these basic "oughts" and "ought nots," we can be led deeper into living out what it truly means to be a human person.

I know it is hard to make an honest assessment of where we are with the Lord. When we do so, we often find out that we already know where we are falling short of the glory of

God! So why not let the light of God's love shine in those dark places in our lives? He already knows where we are struggling and where we are sinning, so our honest examination of ourselves is simply an attempt to offer to Jesus more areas of our lives that need his healing presence.

The encounter with Jesus at Mass should really be unpacked throughout our week as we continue to invite the light of Christ into the secret areas of our lives. This is a life-long process. We may not be able to unlock all those secret places inside us at once. But perhaps you could think of one area of your life that Jesus could enter into. It may be the resentment you have towards the Lord for seemingly not intervening in your life during a particularly difficult time, such as an abusive marriage. It may be your daily struggle with depression and self-hatred, which has led you to despair. Jesus wants to come into these dark areas of your life because he wants you to be free, to be healed, and to be whole.

To be critical about our actions is not the final end or goal here. Rather, it is the honest assessment of our state and the open invitation for Jesus to come and rescue us. It is a way to redirect our efforts, helping us to see where certain paths will lead us if we continue on them and enabling us to counter potential difficulties and solve problems along the way.

Just as the president gives an annual State of the Union address, the spiritual life needs a regular "state of the spirit" address. How are we in our walk with Christ? Jesus wants us to be honest so that we can truly be healed. I hope you can open up a new door in your heart to the love of Christ today. I am excited to see how he tidies up the place!

Prayer Starter: What doors in my heart do I need to open to Jesus?

[2] Thomas Merton, *Conjectures of a Guilty Bystander* (New York: Doubleday Religious Publishing Group, 1968), p. 69.

Caught and Captivated

We need to say yes to God's will for our lives.

Learning from the past is one thing, but fixating on and stewing over things we cannot change from days gone by only lead to spiritual paralysis. That is my tendency. I look back on yesterday and the day before and worry that I should have known better. I think I should be well along in this matter of holiness, but looking back, I find that I am still stumbling out of the gate. It's as if I'll never grow into that glorious oak of strength, forever remaining a small acorn. As I view my past, I can easily become addicted to self-loathing, growing ever more intolerant with my tortoise-like progress in faith.

However, fixating on the past has never helped me be the man of God I need to be for the present. I know this is true, but bad habits are hard to break. To believe that Jesus really does love us and wants to be with us is harder than it seems. That small trip from the head to the heart makes a world of difference when it comes to our actions. I don't want to simply state that I can be a better man by saying yes to Christ's will in my life. Rather, I must move forward with great expectation, believing that he loves me, has forgiven me, and has the best in store for me as I take the next step. To say yes to God's will in my life today may be difficult, but it will affect my tomorrow in a positive way.

If I respond today and then tomorrow to God's will, then I will be more inclined to say yes to his plan the third day. Habitually submitting to the plan of God will have massive repercussions.

Our lives are about a true encounter with Jesus, who has pursued us and wishes to ravish and captivate us with authentic love and acceptance. Think of the passion in the Song of Solomon, the devotion of Hosea to his unfaithful wife, or the tenacity of Jacob longing for his marriage to Rachel and willing to work twice as long to be with his true love. These are small reminders of the love that our Lord has for us. Meditating upon our Lord in the Eucharist can remind us that we are meant to dance with our love, to exchange heartfelt words of love and longing with our Lord, and to know him more and more as lover and spouse.

I will be better tomorrow if I say yes to Christ today, and I will be worse in the future if I remain fixated on the failings of the past. I have one thing to strive and search for in this matter of time, and it must be to allow Christ to catch and captivate me, for he is able to enhance my effort and erase my flaws.

Prayer Starter: Do I fixate too much on the past? How can I say yes to God's will today?

PART FIVE:
GROWING IN CHRIST

Understanding Jesus More Each Day

We have years ahead to grow in Christ.

Many years ago, when my son Kolbe was quite small, he was passing by the large wooden table in our dining room. As he walked by, his older sister handed him a round piece of candy. He began to tap his chest as he marched off into the living room. I asked his sister, "Sarah, did Kolbe just do the Sign of the Cross after eating the candy? Call him back, and let's see if he does it again." Sure enough, upon receiving the candy (albeit with a little prompting, as Sarah handed it to him as if she were a Eucharistic minister), Kolbe did the Sign of the Cross with little taps upon his chest. He was so cute!

This kind of imitation is often the beginning of making something one's own. Kolbe had been going to church his whole life, and it only made sense for him to make the Sign of the Cross after receiving a circular object; it clearly reminded him of what everyone else did each Sunday at Mass. Kolbe has grown into a fine young Catholic man who receives our Lord in the Eucharist every Sunday. He has grown into what it means to be a Catholic and what it means to receive the Eucharist. I think this idea of growth is very important.

As the years pass, we hope that we will become more generous, more loving, and even more aware of what it means for us to receive our Eucharistic Lord. The saints also grew in their understanding of Jesus. We don't begin our spiritual understanding with an infusion of knowledge; rather, we grow into our faith, just as a small child grows into an adult. Growth takes time, and it can even be painful. Your understanding of Jesus in the Eucharist is one that will grow and become very cherished as the years pass. Why? Because just as the people in any healthy, growing relationship learn the beauty of depending upon one another, sharing the good and the bad moments, so too will our relationship with Jesus blossom into something profound as we think of his presence for us in the good and difficult times.

I also think that our growth gives us something to say to those we encounter, both to the friend and to the stranger. What Kolbe said about the Eucharist as a child is nothing close to what he says now as a young man entering his teens. You and I are free to grow deeper in our relationship with Jesus in the Eucharist. We can rest in the fact that we don't begin our spiritual understanding where we eventually end. As we daily grow in Christ, we can speak with confidence of his presence, helping those who, like Kolbe with the candy, still have years of growth ahead of them.

Prayer Starter: How have I grown in my relationship with Christ over the past year? Over the past ten years?

PRACTICE MAKES PERFECT

*Jesus in the Eucharist can help us
choose virtue over vice.*

During certain times of the year, I spend what seems to be an extraordinary amount of time in airports. And it's in those times that I have to struggle to keep my temper under control. The small things drive me crazy, like being singled out to go through the scanning machine (which, to my neurotic mind, screams the arrival of cancer in five years). Likewise, when I am hurrying towards the counter to ask a question about my flight and am slowed down by a man who is moving at a turtle's pace in front of me, I get upset. Why doesn't he realize that I'm in a hurry?

The problem is that over time, I make it a habit of giving in to frustrations and anger, and so it gets easier and easier to do so. Then what once was an occasional state of annoyance becomes a way of life. At a certain point, I have to stop and realize that I have the ability to make choices about how I react in stressful situations. I don't have to become annoyed or angry.

In fact, those little choices are just training ground for the big issues I'll face in my life. If I am in a constant state of irritation and near anger because life isn't kneeling in reverence as I pass by, then I will be more inclined to overreact in any situation—especially in those in which I need to be balanced and calm. Because of yesterday's lack of diligence in battling such behavior, I am more inclined to it in the future.

The principle of habit can work in positive ways as well. The more I respond in a proper manner, the easier it will be for me to do so the next time. The more often a martial arts student runs through the motions of a move, the more fluid, natural, and even second nature that move will become. The more often a person in the military assembles and disassembles his weapon, the more he can do it without even consciously thinking about it. Habits are not always bad ones!

So what does this have to do with faith and, specifically, with living out the Eucharistic love of God? I believe that going to Mass to receive the Eucharist—which for many seems to be a mindless habit that appears to have little to do with how they act throughout the week—really does have an impact on us.

When we choose to meditate on the reality of receiving Jesus in this most intimate way, we develop a habit of holiness over time. The saints practiced spiritual communion when they were unable to literally receive Jesus in the Eucharist. This uniting of their hearts and minds spiritually to the Eucharist helped them grow in their love for Jesus.

Practice makes perfect. The more I am willing to let the Eucharistic Lord into my life, the more I will be able to react with patience and love. How? Because the presence of Christ is a steadfast reminder that there is another way of living this life. As Jesus respectfully treated those who misunderstood him, we have the opportunity to respect those who have no interest in our schedules. As Jesus continued to preach the message of salvation to crowds who were more interested in a quick miracle, we can practice patience when people don't want to hear what we have to say.

It is such an important truth, this lesson of learning how to choose virtue over vice in little things. It isn't a lesson we learn in one moment. Rather, it is one we must regularly remember, practice, and make a part of our lives. A small yes for the good can mean a bigger yes for something great in the future, and, of course, a small yes for a vice can lead to a catastrophic yes in the future. I know that our Lord has a goal for us, and the little steps help us to arrive at this destination.

Prayer Starter: What little choices in my life could I make that would train me for the bigger issues I might face in the future?

The Illusion of Control

The only thing we can really control is whether we decide to trust in the Lord.

So many things are out of our control. What is in our control is whether we bring these difficulties to Jesus. Too often I try to fix what I can't instead of doing the one thing I can.

Part of me wishes that I could will everything to fall in place just the way I see fit. In fact, I often try to do that in matters that pertain to me, as well as in matters that pertain to my children. I want to try and make things fall into place in a way that will help my children have the best possibility for success. But there are many things that I can't control. So many things are beyond our ability to resolve or influence. Thankfully, we are invited by Jesus to offer our worries and cares to him.

Jesus invited all who are weary and heavy laden to come to him and find rest (Matthew 11:28). We are encouraged in the Gospels to focus on the moment and not worry about our past or our future because God does, in fact, care for us (6:25). St. Paul learned how to be content in times of want and in times of plenty (Philippians 4:12). How is that possible? Because St. Paul knew, just as we should know, that God's love for us is what controls that which is beyond our control.

This issue of control really is about trust. If we can begin to trust that Jesus really does care for us and that he invites us to rest in him, especially when we are weak and burdened, then we will be able not only to survive but to find joy in what others find impossible situations. If we trust that Jesus is with us and loves us, then we can recognize that our lack or plentitude isn't based on his fickle affection for us. God loves us, period! This is how we deal with things that are beyond our control: a holy detachment to the things around us and an intentional attachment to God, fostered with prayer. Really, prayer—and trusting that God hears us—is all that we have and all that we can control.

We cannot force a different outcome for many of our circumstances, nor can we manipulate a favorable outcome to a situation that is already negatively resolved. We can depend on Jesus to assist us in those times of difficulties. Prayer will keep our hearts centered on the truth that Christ loves us and is aware of our struggles. Prayer will assist us in remembering that God's love is not intermittent. Prayer fosters the trust and even the holy detachment that we need to be the saints that we are called to be.

When you and I choose to go to Jesus in the Eucharist, whether it is a spiritual communion or actually kneeling before him in church, we are saying with our minds and bodies that we are doing the one thing that is actually under our control. Praying to our Eucharistic Lord is a true acknowledgment that we wish for him to do what we cannot. What he decides is truly up to him, and trust, which is built through the dialogue of prayer, enables us to be content with the outcome.

If we can believe that God is in control and has our best interests at heart, then we can know, regardless of circumstances, that we will be okay. A holy indifference is not something we are born with. It will probably take us most of our lives to learn this one lesson, but it is a worthy endeavor. Let's try and let God do what he does best and trust that his love is the only thing we truly need.

Prayer Starter: What is something in my life beyond my control that I should surrender to the Lord? How can I do that?

Clearing Up the Misunderstandings

You can ask Jesus to help you understand
his presence in the Eucharist.

When he was still a young guy, my son Kolbe approached his mother one afternoon a bit upset. "I don't like Jesus any more," he told her. (Thankfully it was my wife who heard this and not me. I would likely have needed medical attention as I saw my small child on the brink of rejecting his faith!) Linda calmly looked at Kolbe and asked, "Why?" He responded, "Because he doesn't give me a cookie." Kolbe had made up his mind about Jesus because it seemed that everyone else but him was able to get a "cookie" after sitting so patiently at Mass.

Trying to communicate to a little boy that what he thinks is a cookie is actually Jesus in the Eucharist is no small task! Linda did what she could to explain it, and since our role in his life is to be the primary catechists for our children, hooray for us! When I say "us," of course I mean my wife, but I've decided to include myself in this parenting success.

Not long after hearing about this story, I was at Mass with my family, and we were kneeling before our Lord. I honestly can't tell you what I was thinking at the time, but I will never forget this moment as long as I live. Kolbe was kneeling next to me. Looking at the priest as he held up the large Host,

Kolbe said with awe and in a hushed voice, "That's a big cookie!" Alas, more catechesis was apparently needed!

I have found such encouragement over the years in telling this story. The truth of Jesus in the Eucharist is there when we completely understand his presence before us or when we get it wrong. We don't have to have everything figured out right away. But we should know that Christ is committed to bringing us closer to him.

Believing in Jesus' presence in the Eucharist can be a stumbling block due to past misunderstandings or unfortunate circumstances in our lives. Maybe we have struggled with seeing God as a Father who is actually loving and available because we had absent or abusive parents. Maybe we have a difficult time seeing Jesus as a friend and elder brother in the faith because of the betrayal of a friend or sibling. Whatever the problem or misunderstanding, Jesus can walk us away from an unhealthy perspective and into a healthy one. To grow in our faith sometimes involves looking again at Jesus and asking the question "Why?" Why am I hesitant to believe that he is there before me? Why am I afraid that he doesn't know what I am going through? Why do I feel like Jesus is always angry with me?

Asking those questions will enable us to replace misinformation with positive truth. As our needs become articulated and as our misunderstandings become known, we will grow in awareness of the reality of who Jesus is. He doesn't shake his head, disappointed because we've misunderstood him once again. Rather, he lovingly waits for us to hear him speak healing into our brokenness and strength into our weaknesses.

When little Kolbe mistook the consecrated Host for a cookie, I didn't get angry with him even though he had already been told that it was Jesus in the Eucharist. It was understandable—this was, after all, a kid who loves cookies! Likewise, it is understandable for you to struggle with some of the misunderstandings you have about Jesus because of where you are on your spiritual journey. Be attentive to your concerns and questions when you are talking with the Lord. Be aware of your hesitations and worries, and ask the question "Why?" The answer may not be clear right away, but you can ask Jesus to open your heart so that you can understand and see him more clearly each day.

Your appreciation of Jesus will influence what you say about him to those you work with and live with. If you find Jesus difficult to approach, then you won't invite your friends to run to him when they hurt. If you feel Jesus is distant, then you won't readily offer him as the solution to their pain. He is waiting to help you know him more today!

Prayer Starter: What questions should I ask Jesus to help clear up misunderstandings I have of him?

Relationship Begets Action

Every action we take should be informed by our relationship with Jesus.

Our relationship with Jesus should show up not only in our demeanor but also in our actions. We shouldn't just talk about Christ; we should use our actions to witness to that relationship.

Here is an example of what I am talking about. Because we are married, my wife and I don't go around flirting with others. Our relationship is nourished and encouraged, and the reminder of who we are together helps us to live our lives in faithfulness even when we are not in the same physical location. Our walk with Jesus in the Eucharist should similarly affect our actions—how we interact with the world, how we order our passions, and how we protect ourselves against the lies of the enemy.

The relationship we have with the Eucharist today is probably different than it was a few years ago, but that is a good thing. No one would say that their marriage stays the same every single year. You grow into what it means to love, sacrifice for, and serve one another. Your relationship can start out quite passionate and exciting, but the love is real even when the passion fades and the difficulties are exhausting.

Even with changes and struggles, our marital love is not only present but enhanced. This is the same with our walk with Jesus. It might start out with the initial newness and excitement of having found him, but over time it really becomes integrated with the daily rhythms of our lives. We should all remember how blessed we are to receive Jesus, and the gift of intimacy with him should show up in a joy-filled reality. But even in difficult times, we can still know the love of Christ is present, enhancing and enriching the relationship.

We must, of course, live in a way that shows what we will and won't do because of our relationship with Jesus. But if we are not careful to foster the union with genuine actions, we will become the person who is just going through the motions. Truly live out the love that you profess!

Prayer Starter: How do my actions show that I have a relationship with Jesus?

BUILDING UP MUSCLES OF TRUST

The more trust we can place in Jesus, the less worrying
we have to do for ourselves!

I know we are not supposed to worry about things, but I'm so good at it! If you're like me (and I say that knowing that you're probably not that far gone yet), then it seems as if worry is something we didn't have to learn. Rather, it was just something that we've unpacked over the years. Maybe I'm trying to prove to Jesus that I'm taking things seriously. "See, Jesus, I am not letting this go, and my tenacity in thinking about this issue is proof positive that I truly care." While this is very understandable, I have a better solution to show God that I am serious about this worrisome matter.

Let's take a son who is now in high school and nearing graduation as an example. We have raised that son the best way we could, and now he is journeying off into the uncharted waters of collegiate life. That child has learned right from wrong and has realized that there is a cause and effect to his actions. Knowing that we did our job and that he is a great kid doesn't mean that we don't worry about him. Some of that is normal, and I would say that it is more an expression of being concerned than worry, but the two can often blur.

Let's imagine that I promised you that I would personally watch over your child at all moments to assist him when needed and to protect him. If that is of no comfort to you, then substitute someone you know and trust! In reality, Jesus, as well as that child's guardian angel, the saints, and our Lady, all have his sanctity in mind. As we ask all of heaven to come and be present with him, we begin to counter worry with a viable and authentic solution.

How do we know that Jesus will be there for our children? Because he is there for us, daily and constantly in the Eucharist. Jesus' presence ensures that he truly cares for us. Remember when Jesus speaks about the flowers being adorned in beauty and a sparrow not falling without the Lord knowing it (Matthew 6:28; 10:29-30)? He says we are of greater value than many sparrows (10:31). Does this mean that bad things never happen to good people? Of course not! But we can know that Jesus' presence will be enough to keep us steady. Remember Jesus walking on the water during the storm (Mark 6:45-52)?

If you do not find yourself building the "muscles" of trust, it will be very difficult for you to not rely on the old habit of worrying. After all, you've been building the worry muscle most of your life. Jesus comes and quietly invites you to give to him your children, your awkward moments, your dreams and fears, and asks you to trust that he cares about them more than you do. You haven't proved a thing by obsessing over these issues, except that you are not trusting Jesus yet with your problem. That's what we emphatically declare when we worry: "Jesus, I don't trust you to take this from me."

It is a little yes each day that will enable you to build the muscles of trust. As you trust Jesus for the tiny things in your life, his faithfulness will be a source of confidence when you face the large things in life. Think about David as he faced Goliath. David was confident that God would give him the victory over this proven warrior. Why? Because God had given him victory over the lions and other predators who came to destroy the sheep he was tending (1 Samuel 17:36-37). Because God had been present and had given him victory over these smaller foes, David trusted that God would absolutely give him victory over this Philistine who had so greatly offended the armies of the God of Israel.

If we want to learn how to lighten the load of worry in our lives, then we have to begin to grow in our trust of Christ. It won't be an immediate fix because, again, worrying is something we are good at and used to, but over time we will start to realize that Jesus' love for us, his constant presence to us in the Eucharist, is proof that when he commits himself to something, he means business. In the words of the classic song from so long ago, "Don't Worry, Be Happy." Why? Because Jesus really does care for you more than you can ever imagine. Trust me. Well, actually—trust him!

Prayer Starter: What is one worry that I can entrust to God today?

Learning to Be Thankfully Dependent

If we want to be people of thanksgiving,
we have to learn to rely on him.

We don't generally look upon the idea of dependence as a virtue. We want to be independent, for crying out loud! But the ideal scenario for us on this journey of faith is to be thankfully dependent. We have our whole lives to learn that lesson.

Of course, Jesus won't force us to trust him. He gives us freedom so that we can choose to love him. So we have to choose to grow in faith, and this is where it can get a little odd, because your choice must be a dependence upon Jesus. It seems to be a paradox—choosing to depend upon someone other than yourself—but that is what guarantees a heart of thanksgiving. If you do not depend and trust that Christ loves and wants the best for you, then difficult moments can become a petri dish of discontent, resentment, and frustration. And we have to choose to rely and depend upon Jesus, not only in moments of difficulty, but also in times when we feel as if we have it all figured out.

When we find ourselves in a difficult situation, even if we got into it gradually, we often want God to rescue us immediately. Sometimes he does, but more often than not, he rescues us gradually. The process matters, because we have the opportunity to trust and depend on him throughout the whole time. Our faith isn't like fast food; rather, it is a relationship in which we learn what love looks like in good times and in bad.

The irony is that while we usually want to be independent and make our own decisions, when things don't go our way, we want to blame someone other than ourselves. If we are choosing to trust and depend upon Jesus with our families and our struggles, then when something doesn't go our way, we can and must be thankful to Jesus that he is in charge. This willingness to give Jesus the "benefit of the doubt" is a choice too, by the way. "Jesus, I trust you to get me the position I am applying for, the raise that I am due, the days off that I desperately need." If I trust that Jesus sees the big picture and has my sanctity in mind and the best interests of my family and me at heart, then if I don't get the position, the pay raise, or the vacation days, I can still rest in thanksgiving that I have not been forgotten.

You and I have a choice today: will we thankfully depend upon Jesus for our needs and wants, or will we try to do things our own way? We will be faced with many opportunities to depend on Jesus, whether we are experiencing want or plenty. It is a lesson we all need to learn, and for that I am thankful!

Prayer Starter: How has my dependence on Jesus made me thankful?

Jesus' Hidden Years

Jesus serving us in the Eucharist should be the example of service that we ourselves live out.

God is a family of complete gift from one Person to the other. While we can talk about this Trinity forever, our words will never articulate perfectly the finality of God's self-existence. But so that we don't have to guess about the meaning of love, the Second Person of the Blessed Trinity became flesh, and Jesus showed us what that complete self-giving, that heavenly *agape* love, looks like in time.

And what do we see from studying the life of Jesus? We see that real love is sacrificial; it is service oriented, mediatory, and demonstrated by advocating for others. Jesus uses his two natures, divine and human, to show us what love really is, how it looks and works, and why we must be enveloped in it. If Jesus is one Person, and in fact he is, with two natures (human and divine), then how he loves others, what it looks like, and its gift to humanity should make all the difference in our lives.

That's why understanding the Person of Jesus Christ is of the utmost importance for us. Because we are Christians and therefore followers of Christ, it is something that we need to do. What we understand about Jesus comes primarily from the Gospels. But what we don't get from any of the Gospel writers is anything about Jesus' early years, specifically from age thirteen until he begins his public ministry at age thirty. However, who Jesus was in his public ministry is very much present and unfolding in his hidden years.

For example, Jesus served those around him by making the blind see, the deaf hear, and the lame walk. In the feeding with the fish and loaves, he even made sure that the people had their need for food fulfilled, and at the wedding at Cana, he made sure that a couple avoided shame and embarrassment. We can be certain that these acts of love and selflessness were also something that Jesus did in his hidden years as a young man.

Think about Jesus serving Mary and Joseph. I'll bet it was a glorious time of trying to outdo one another in sacrificial love. I can imagine Jesus waking up early to help Mary with the housework before leaving with St. Joseph to assist him as a carpenter. I can see him picking up the wood or stone that fell from their workbench so that Joseph could avoid straining his back. It would be in line with Jesus' character to see him talking with an elderly woman or getting her a drink of water, or holding the hand of someone who was sick and hurting. I am confident that he would have always found a way to make other people around him feel more important. He would have given them the best place to sit and would have treated them with dignity and respect.

Jesus would have certainly been obedient to his elders, even if he felt like doing something else. He would have regularly offered himself to others, sacrificing what he might otherwise want, to be present to another's need. I am sure that as a child, Jesus "stood in the gap" for others who were being picked on, and I'll bet that he made the most convincing argument for doing the right thing when his friends wanted him to join them in doing something wrong. I am sure that there were times when he turned the other cheek and possibly gave his tunic when someone stole his cloak.

I know that Jesus longs to serve you in the Eucharist in the same way. When you come to him sick or with great sorrow and need, Jesus is ready to be present with you. As a result, you too are given the chance to go and serve your family and friends. The more we meditate upon the life of Jesus, the more we can live this out in the real world.

When you spend time with Jesus in the Eucharist, it is an opportunity for you to embrace the sacrificial gift of Jesus and imitate him in your daily encounters. If you find yourself looking for ways to sacrifice for another, I am confident that you are on your way to living out the Eucharist. Staying a little longer to help clean up after a party, reading an extra chapter of a book to a child who is ready for bed, or just picking up around the house without being asked are all ways to live out the sacrificial love of the Eucharist. As Jesus "stood in the gap" for us at Calvary, we have the same opportunity; we can fight for what is right or just, even if it means that we will pay a high price. The Eucharist among us is truly Jesus reminding us that even now, his example of humility is the way we can most show the world what love looks like.

While the hidden years of Jesus are often enveloped in mystery, I am sure we wouldn't be surprised for one minute if everything that happened in those years became known to us. Jesus' love changed the world, and to this day, we feel the embrace of such genuine love. We can share this love with others. We must share it! Today is your day to truly let Christ move in and through you. Let's not keep his sacrificial love a secret.

Prayer Starter: How can I better live out the sacrificial love of Jesus? What opportunities do I have to "stand in the gap" for someone?

Our Duty to Give Thanks

God's gift in the Eucharist turns even the most difficult
moments into an opportunity to give thanks.

It is truly right and just, our duty and our salvation, always and everywhere to give you thanks, Father most holy, through your beloved Son, Jesus Christ." As part of Eucharistic Prayer II, these are familiar words to most of us. While it is easy to mumble the phrase without much thought, it is worth taking a moment to consider the choice of words placed within this liturgical sentence.

Without a doubt, it is not only right but also just to give the Father thanks. In fact, it is a matter of justice. Justice is one of the four cardinal virtues (the others are prudence, temperance, and fortitude) that gives to God and man that which they deserve. To treat every human person with dignity and respect, regardless of their age, color, or gender, is to practice justice. Many other virtues hinge upon the four cardinal ones. It is easier to recognize the importance of treating one another with respect than it is to understand the importance of justice in how we approach God. Yet our role is to be just to both man and God.

How do we give God that which is due him? It is impossible to fully repay God for all that he has done since he is the author of all that is. That being said, being a person of thanksgiving is a way that we can fulfill justice towards a God who is worthy of our praise. And within the context of the Mass, we can truly give what is right and just to God.

Uttering constant prayers of gratitude to God is of great importance—after all, St. Paul said that we are to give thanks to God in everything, for it is God's will for us (1 Thessalonians 5:18). But joining in the Eucharist is the pinnacle of thanksgiving. If we long to have an authentic heart of thanksgiving, we must unite our gratitude with Jesus Christ's salvific work. "Through your beloved Son, Jesus Christ" is how we fulfill our thanksgiving to God, which is our duty. Our duty is wrapped up in this gratitude, which is exponentially increased; we know that we are doing what we were made to do. If we do what is right, being people of justice, fulfilling our duty to God by always and everywhere giving him thanks, specifically through Jesus Christ, then we will be the recipients of his salvation!

This saving gift is given to us at Mass, and that is why—always and everywhere—we continue to participate in the Eucharistic meal. When St. Paul said that we should be thankful in everything, he didn't mean that we have to muster this thankfulness by ourselves. Rather, he said, in everything we can give thanks, for it is the will of God in Christ Jesus for us. "In Christ" is a phrase that St. Paul uses a lot. To be the people of thanksgiving that we are called to be, we must seize the opportunity to truly unite our lives with Jesus Christ, making our sufferings redemptive and grounding our joys in his salvation.

We have good days and bad days, but Jesus comes to us in

the Eucharist on all of them. If we can unite ourselves to the Father through the Son at Mass, then our difficult circumstances can become occasions of gratitude. If we can bring our concerns to the Eucharist, we can rejoice even in the storms of life. Jesus wants our hearts to be grateful, and while it is just for us to give praise and honor back to God, we are given the best possible opportunity for success: uniting our thanksgiving to the sacrifice of Jesus. Because of the Mass, we do the impossible. We give back to God that which he is due! On our own, we wouldn't be able to fulfill this virtue of justice. But in Christ, in doing our just duty, we can give thanks. Thank God!

Prayer Starter: How often do I unite my thanksgiving to the sacrifice of Jesus at Mass? How would it change my experience of Mass if I did so?

Part Six:
The Family of God

True Friendship

We gather together at Mass with friends and saints.

One morning after I dropped my kids off at school, I made my way into church for Mass. A few minutes after I had settled into the pew, a wonderful friend sat down beside me. He brought a smile to my face. I love his family, his consistent pursuit of Christ, and his deep and profound insights concerning the faith. Our kids play baseball together, and we try to gather our families together for dinners and fellowship whenever possible. Then, a few minutes later, another close friend slipped in next to me with his adopted son. Things were getting crowded now!

This collection of friends and family is the beauty of loving the Eucharist. Christ gathers us together from all walks of life in order to share a holy meal with us. Just as a family gathering can bring wonderful memories, build unity, and enhance fellowship, so even more can the uniting reality of the Eucharist affirm and strengthen friendships.

Jesus said that there is no greater love than that of a friend who willingly lays down his life for another (John 15:13). Friendship is important, and our earthly friendships should model the love that Christ has for us. "There is a friend who sticks closer than a brother" (Proverbs 18:24), and that friend is Jesus. As both friend and brother, Jesus shows us what it means to truly befriend another in the context of an authentic family relationship. Our relationship with Jesus in the Eucharist should speak and witness to us a practical way of befriending those within our reach.

Right before I went to Mass that morning, I had tweeted to my online friends that I would be praying for them that day. "Sending up prayers for you all at Mass this morning. You are not forgotten nor alone." There are many people who follow me on Twitter whom I may have met only once or know of me only through my music, writing, or talks. One woman wrote back to me, "I *needed* to see that this morning." Our experience of Christ in the Eucharist can even touch people who are not in our closest circle of friends. It is profound to realize that Jesus invites us to befriend not only our closest companions whom we have grown to love and cherish but also the stranger.

Similarly, the communion I have with those who are already in the beatific vision is of great importance for my daily life. These saints, many of whom we know—and many more whom we don't—continue to pray and cheer us on as we journey into the arms of Jesus. St. Elizabeth Ann Seton has been like a family friend for many years. She helped us as we made the decision to put our kids in Catholic schools. She is also very present in my prayers for my family, many of whom are teachers. I believe that these heavenly friends are always ready to assist us in love.

We all gather together at Mass! All the saints are our friends, and because of this reality, we are never alone. Their heavenly friendship is given so that we on earth, without reserve, can be a friend to those around us. Your love for the Eucharist may make attending Mass a little more crowded, but I have a feeling that's a good thing! Let us be to others what Christ is to us in the Eucharist: a true friend.

Prayer Starter: Is there anyone I know who might be in need of a true friend?

Bringing Jesus to Others

We can invest in those who don't know the Lord.

Have you ever noticed how crowded church is on Ash Wednesday? You may not see some people for months on end, but the moment that Ash Wednesday arrives, they flock to the church to get ashes—and then they leave, not even staying until the end of Mass!

But Ash Wednesday is about the Eucharist, not about the ashes. Beyond the reminder of our mortality with the ashes upon our foreheads is the reception of Christ in the Eucharist, which is the ultimate reminder that we are no longer our own and will one day be with God.

We have to ask ourselves why they aren't staying. The problem may be that we have probably not spent a lot of time talking about how important and practical the Eucharist is in our everyday lives.

How do we welcome them back? The answer isn't to jazz up the liturgy to compete with the neighboring church with the larger budget and the high-tech equipment. But maybe we should increase our personal outreach efforts. Maybe we can care for people in a way that is a little outside the box.

I think that more people will come to Mass and stay if parishioners are falling in love with Jesus. Trying to find ways to teach the truth about the Eucharist to our youth and our adults should be on the top of our list. I have found that if we can somehow get people to take a step out of their comfort zones and begin to learn again (as adults) or for the first time (as youth) the beauty of our Lord, then their relationship with Jesus begins to blossom.

We can't assume that our kids—or many adults, for that matter—have already been captivated by the heart of Jesus. If we bring people Jesus and if we really care about those people, investing what we have with a lot of love and care, it can be the beginning of a beautiful romance.

Prayer Starter: Do I take the time to invest in someone and so bring that person to Jesus?

Speaking the Truth in Love

The Lord might have a difficult word for you to share.

It's often difficult to speak the truth in love to our friends and families. Such words can be difficult to both give and accept. But doing so enhances the virtue of humility in both the one who is speaking those words and the one who is hearing them. In fact, we do not love our neighbor when we fail to speak charitable words of correction when necessary.

Here's a recent example from my own life. I travel often for musical performances, retreats, and youth conferences, and when I am home, I have to teach three university classes. Fulfilling these obligations with perfect fluidity, along with meeting writing deadlines and the various demands of a large family, has been about as easy as juggling cats. One Sunday my wife and I got everyone loaded into two vehicles and made it to church. I'd arrived home the night before and was trying to catch up on bills, chores, and so forth, and as a result, I slept in later than I should have that Sunday morning. Given my traveling schedule, it's rare for me to attend Sunday Mass with my family, so I was happy to help my wife with the kids at church before I had to go to the airport for my next trip that afternoon. Sometimes a half day at home is a cherished grace!

I was wearing some pretty tattered jeans that morning and didn't really think about it as we got into the car. While

I was at Mass, I looked down at the tattered denim and thought, "Good grief, these pants have pretty much had it." In fact, I felt a bit embarrassed wearing them to church. As I was making my way out of the church at the end of Mass, a friend and colleague approached me. After greeting me, he said that while he didn't really care if I wore jeans to church, I probably should not wear ones that were so tattered. He assured me that he was in no way perfect—he thought his own sins made him more tattered than my pants—but he also thought that it was important to mention it to me.

I felt crushed. I tried to articulate my insane schedule and then just finally stated that I was thinking the same thing. It was really a confirmation that while Jesus sure does love me just the way I am, I am certainly lacking in the clothing department. I thanked him and readily agreed that it was, in fact, time for the pants to go. As we finished up our brief chat, he remarked, "That was easy."

It may have been that he was stewing about whether to even mention this to me at all. How would I take the criticism? Would it come across as a pride-filled comment on his behalf? While his words to me were hard to hear, I had to agree with him, and in the end, I think it showed that our friendship was probably more real than if he had stayed silent.

When you invite Jesus deeper into your life each Eucharist, it is possible that the Lord will give you a difficult word to bring to another. You will need a lot of love and grace to mention this weakness in a way that comes across as humble and sincere. I don't see it as our job to become someone's clothing police or to try to nitpick each and every flaw that a person has. But there will be times when the Lord puts people in our lives who can benefit from an honest word.

It will take humility on your part to share it and humility on their part to receive it. It will require your obedience to God as well as your love for your neighbor. You won't be able to control how they respond, but your words could just be an affirmation of what the Lord is already saying to them, just as it was for me!

Prayer Starter: When someone speaks a word of truth to me, how do I react? How can I grow in humility and be eager to receive words of correction?

Love the Sinner

*The love of Christ in the Eucharist is the
motivation we need to change.*

One day a distraught mother from Boston approached me and said that her daughter was a drug addict. This woman's life had been very difficult as she tried to deal with her child's messy and heart-wrenching struggle. Yet she was going home that night to tell her daughter that she loves her—period—even if she doesn't break her drug addiction.

That's the kind of amazing love that Jesus has for us. We hold grudges; we fulfill disordered passions; we often struggle with jealousy, indifference, envy, pride, and the like—and yet Christ's love is stronger than all of these sinful things. And when we show someone the unconditional love of God even in spite of that person's sin, as the woman from Boston did, it doesn't mean that we are condoning what they have done. It also doesn't necessarily lead the person being loved to automatically justify their sin.

In fact, I believe unconditional love will do the opposite—it will lead the individual to long for a holier life. I love the person who is sinful; I love him or her whether they illicitly act upon a disordered passion or not—period! Receiving that kind of love, which flows from God, motivates us toward a holy life, a life that is truly authentic and not bound by the chains of sin.

When the woman in Boston told me about her daughter, I didn't say, "Okay, but make sure you let her know that you don't approve of her sin." Good grief! Haven't we already tried this subtle, judgmental type of "love" before? We know how it usually ends. Think about your own life. Why did you ever change your behavior—I mean, really change? Most of us knew what we needed to know about being a good Christian from Sunday school and from our parents, but how did we really choose to change? A healthy motivation is the key to a lasting change in behavior.

The Eucharist gives us the motivation we need because it is truly a Person we encounter. That Person is in love with us. And as St. John said, "We love, because he first loved us" (1 John 4:19). We need the motivation of Jesus so that we can live differently. We have tried and failed so many times. Yet Jesus looks at us and says, "You are accepted." Jesus is ready to enable us to change, but he wants it to last. Our motivation must be him, not just our trying to please him. Why? Because he is already pleased with us. I know that seems hard to believe, but it is true! We are already loved, and now we can rest in his love and extend it to others.

We also need the motivation of Christ so that we can offer forgiveness to those who have hurt us, just as Jesus on the cross forgave those who had been mercilessly brutal towards him (Luke 23:34). How often have we been forgiven? I am thinking it is more than seven or even more than seventy times seven. Who has offended you? Who has sinned against you? I wonder if you could be a motivation for another's change. Your forgiveness, extended to someone who has hurt you, will be a Eucharistic moment bringing a thankful heart both to you and the sinner you have forgiven.

We have the chance this week, this day, this minute, to love people who have sinned. These sinners are often our sisters and brothers, our parents and friends, not someone far away. The Eucharist changes us. Jesus loves us just the way we are, and it is his love that motivates our change. Receiving blessings such as forgiveness can be rare and often a surprise, but giving blessings is never an accident. These moments of giving blessings and offering forgiveness can and must be repeated often. Be someone's surprise today! Love the sinner.

Prayer Starter: Whom do I need to love and forgive with the unconditional love of God?

PART SEVEN:
OUR CALLING AND DESTINY

WE ARE EUCHARISTIC PEOPLE

We get to be Jesus to the people we meet everyday.

There have been many well-documented Eucharistic miracles, especially when suddenly the "accidents" of bread and wine miraculously disappear and we behold the substance of the Lord's flesh and blood. Jesus is truly present, body, blood, soul, and divinity, even when the accidents remain, but a number of reported cases have occurred in which people can go and see the flesh, such as the Eucharistic miracle of Lanciano, Italy. While these are special and certainly cause us to respond with a greater sensitivity when visiting such devotional sites, we would do well to remember that Jesus is truly with us at every Mass and in a unique way in each of us as we leave our parishes each Sunday.

During the consecration at Mass, the whole substance of the bread and wine is changed into the substance of the Body of Jesus, our Lord. We call his "transubstantiation" (*Catechism of the Catholic Church*, 1376). (In some traditions, such as Lutheranism, Jesus is believed to be present along with bread and wine. That is called "consubstantiation," but it is not what Catholics acknowledge Jesus Christ to have instituted at the Last Supper.)

After the Mass, the celebrant takes the remaining consecrated Hosts and places them back into the tabernacle. Why? So we can reverence and adore our Lord. The change of mere bread and wine into the true presence of Jesus cannot be revoked or evaporate. A true change has occurred, whether we realize it or not!

Through baptism, the true presence of Christ has also changed us. In fact, baptism ontologically changes us. We are not the same individuals we were because of Christ's presence in us, and regardless of whether people notice it or not, baptism makes us new creatures in Christ. The mark of baptism is as permanent as circumcision was for the Jewish males in the Old and New Testaments. In many ways, we are a profound miracle. The way God can take average flesh and bone and make it into something holy and even saintly is something beyond our abilities. We are united with Christ in baptism and given a chance to go out and bring that love to the world around us. Others who are unaware of the impact Christ has had in our lives may not reverence us, and this shouldn't surprise us. We must remember that many do not reverence the Eucharist, and certainly many continue to lack devotion to Jesus, just as they did in the Gospels.

What I want to leave you with is this simple truth: we are Eucharistic people! The source and summit of our faith find their culmination in the Eucharist, and this must show in how we live. We might look like mere mortals, average Joes and Janes, but because of Christ, we get to be the transforming presence of Christ to those who will never walk into a church. We get to wipe the tears of a frustrated child and carry the burdens of a stressed-out friend or family member.

Because of Christ's transformative work in our lives, we can be a healing presence to the embittered employee and consolation to the distraught and downhearted. We get to be Jesus to those we meet every day.

For those who have been touched by Christ in us and through us, we become the miracle they need. I suppose it really is a surprise that God could use any one of us to help another in their time of need, and he certainly could have done it a different way. But God in his wisdom saw that it was fitting for you and me to carry his presence into the world. What an exciting opportunity to allow the change Christ has done in us to initiate a change in those we encounter!

While Eucharistic miracles are often rare, I do hope that we, as Eucharistic people, are not such a rarity in such times as these. I hope that every city and every parish has dozens of people, even hundreds, who will go out and show Christ to the world in powerful and dramatic ways. I pray that we stun and cause wonder and awe to many by our willingness to reflect and witness to Christ in us. God knows our limitations, but he is all about doing the miraculous, even with people like you and me.

Prayer Starter: When have I carried the presence of Jesus to another? To whom can I show the face of Christ today?

THE INEXPLICABLE EUCHARIST

*You don't need to be able to explain it—
just respond in faith.*

There are many attributes that we can use to discuss God, but all of them pale in comparison with the reality of who he is. If I say that God is great or, better still, that he is love, that is a true statement. But what is contained in that sentiment is nothing in comparison with the reality. God is not *like* love; he *is* love. Any description of love in our poetry, stories, or even experiences is just a simple particle of his grandeur.

We could also say that God is good. But it isn't as if God holds a greater portion of goodness compared to any created being; rather, he *is* goodness. He is the attribute but also beyond the fullness of its definition. In fact, we could say that the definition of goodness is so lacking in its actual comparison to God that it is more dissimilar than similar. It seems impossible to describe the indescribable, yet still we fumble with words in order to try and convey the greatness of our God. Even our best articulation will pale in comparison to the reality.

While this is true, God intentionally reveals himself to us throughout the economy of salvation and ultimately in the Person of Jesus Christ. What was learned through the various stages of God's revelation was ultimately revealed in

Jesus, who is the invisible God made visible in all his deity in bodily form. Jesus did not belittle our understanding of God by his thirty-plus years of living among us. Jesus doesn't ask that we describe who he is before we can be accepted into his salvific work. We can stumble into Jesus' presence and, like the woman caught in the act of adultery, find forgiveness from the One worthy of condemning us (John 8:1-11). We are like the leper who was unclean (Matthew 8:1-4). We are like Zacchaeus who was despised because he was a tax collector (Luke 19:1-10), and yet Jesus comes and heals us, even offering to come to our own heart, which is our home.

This encounter with Jesus is beyond our ability to articulate. We find ourselves in the presence of Christ in these Scripture stories, and yet we still run up against the limitations of our language to truly express what we are seeing and experiencing. Can you imagine the relief of the woman caught in the act of adultery or the joy in hearing Jesus say he is coming to your house?

When we talk about the Eucharist, it is often the case that we struggle with limitations in our language to describe what we are feeling, experiencing, and encountering. When our heart catches a glimpse of him, we are at a loss. This is the mystery of the Incarnation: how can God become man? How can Jesus look like bread? When you and I find ourselves gazing at the Eucharist with an inability to communicate to others why we must go and adore our Lord, it is probable that others will not understand.

When his disciples felt the need to leave their families in order to go and follow Jesus Christ two thousand years ago, I am sure that people didn't understand. Jesus' love for humanity is so radical and inexplicable that he allowed people to misunderstand that the Second Person of the Blessed Trinity was in their midst. He wanted nothing more for them than that they believe his message, embrace his Father, and follow him completely, but he also knew that he could not coerce them.

Today Jesus is still misunderstood, ignored, and even overtly mocked because he still offers each one of us a chance to freely respond to his presence in the Eucharist. We may not be able to fully articulate why we have left wealth and status in order to be counted among his followers, but we can echo Simon Peter when he said, "Lord, to whom shall we go? You have the words of eternal life" (John 6:68). We may not be able to share with others much more than that, but I think that may be enough.

Prayer Starter: How can I explain the Eucharist to someone? Is there anyone with whom I can share my love of the Eucharist today?

The Greatness That Awaits Us

*The Eucharist helps us to understand the
limitlessness of our souls.*

While we might imagine what it would be like to travel through time and space instantaneously, most of us are not capable of such a feat. I can't be at my daughter's soccer game and my son's football game at the same time. I would love to, but when I head over to the soccer match, I inevitably miss the drama taking place on the football field.

When Jesus, the Second Person of the Blessed Trinity, became flesh, he willingly took upon himself the limitations of time and space. Jesus was present in a specific location at one time. For Jesus, of course, there were exceptions to the steadfast rules of time and space, but God's grace was working and building upon the natural realities. His acts were done at a certain time, day or evening, during one feast or near another.

Within the limitations of time and space, Jesus gave us hints of what power he had outside of natural restrictions. He made deaf ears hear and blind eyes see, and for the vast majority of us, that is certainly beyond our greatest acts or deeds. We don't know how much the Second Person limited himself in the confines of time and space because we don't know how limitless he ultimately is outside of these confines.

We see dimly here, in our world, as St. Paul reminds us (1 Corinthians 13:12). We are unable to conceive of anything that our imaginations can't foster.

Jesus confined himself to the limitations of time and space back then, and this is also the case with the Eucharist. He can be with everyone here in this world, to be sure, but he is specifically present in the Eucharist. In the tabernacles around the world, at every Mass that is celebrated, at each opportunity for Eucharistic adoration, Jesus comes to us, truly, in a way that is subject to the realities of time and space. Grace is building and working within the natural realities so that we can begin to understand more about our God. We will never be able to grasp the enormity of the supernatural becoming natural within time and space, and yet we do get a glimpse of this with our own mortality.

We know of a friend who has cancer, who any day now will pass into eternity. There have been thousands of friends on Facebook who have promised their prayers and support for this family. I've been thinking about the beauty of our Church and how strangers, upon hearing about this woman, are praying for someone they don't even know. The momentum has been growing in these final days, as more and more people tune in to the sorrow of the family, who have made themselves vulnerable by allowing others to watch them prepare to send off their beloved wife and mother. But this demonstration of thousands praying is only a fraction of the body of Christ in eternity that I imagine is reaching into the room of this one so close to death. All of heaven is eagerly reaching out to her, and in some small way, it's as if the earth willingly relents to the limitlessness of eternity so that the two can connect.

Just as we struggle to grasp the enormity of Jesus taking on a human nature, limiting himself in time and space to be like us, so we also are unable to comprehend the limitlessness of a soul, which has been confined to the bodily limitations of space and time but someday will be entering into eternity. As our friend dies, the restrictions are loosened. We have no idea how free one becomes in the embrace of the limitlessness of God's love, but we do know that it will be a continual source of satisfaction and beauty.

How can we really know what greatness awaits us? We can't, except by juxtaposing the reality of God's entrance into time as a man. The more we meditate upon the profound humility of Jesus in the Eucharist, the more we can begin to understand that conversely, we will become in Christ greater demonstrations of who we are than we could have previously imagined. We will no longer be hindered by sinful inclinations or the weight of sorrow and disappointments. Christ Jesus shows us his willingness to transform our understanding of what simply is to what can and will be.

Prayer Starter: When I meditate on the profound humility of Jesus in the Eucharist, how does this help me understand what greatness awaits me in the future?

No Quick Fixes

Jesus is with us, however long it takes.

Too often we become intolerant with the time it takes us to rid ourselves of our imperfections. As a result of this endless list of inadequacies and messiness, we resort to quick fixes, pat answers, and fortune-cookie slogans that sound just right but are unable to carry us through the entirety of our journey. At times we polish the authenticity right out of the gospel. The good news is not that we have become rid of the flesh and its demands, or the world and its barrage of intolerance, or the silencing of the devil and his lying minions. Rather, it is the confidence that we have been "bought with a price" (1 Corinthians 7:23); we are no longer our own, so the worry and concern for ourselves now rests upon Jesus Christ and not our shoulders. This exchange is a necessity if we are to really be the embodiment of thanksgiving!

When we pass by a church, whether it is a majestic structure or a utilitarian sanctuary, Jesus is in the tabernacle, waiting to encounter us all. Christ remains present for the mother processing the loss of a child, the senior agonizing with the loneliness of life, the student wrestling with angst and stress, and the young man or woman in turmoil, trying to discern their vocation. Among all of the changes we face, Jesus is still waiting, still present, and still willing to be in our lives.

The stability of Jesus in the Eucharist should bring great hope. The time it will take for us to become saints is exactly the time that remains before us, no more and no less. Jesus' constancy in our lives is an invitation to lean brokenly upon the Person of Jesus Christ, who has a heart that beats for our daily growth. There is no magic phrase that we can mutter that will make us holy.

Why are we afraid of this process? I think it is because we don't want to wait for anything. If it can't happen quickly, then it is of little significance to us. Yet the formation of mountains and valleys, the redwoods and the Grand Canyon, the stars in the sky, and the development of a human life all take time. Have we superimposed a fast-food consumer mentality into our Christianity, thinking that today it is more relevant? If so, we are going to be sorely mistaken when all our problems haven't vanished since our last confession or even since our baptism.

We get to grow into spiritual maturity, allowing Christ into the next moment of this habitation of time and space. I think this is one of the true treasures that we can hold onto from our interaction with the Eucharist: that he is with us for the entirety of our journey, both here and now and in eternity. How much more should that motivate us to be present to others around us? We have the chance to be Eucharistic people, and in fact we are, so extending patience and sensitivity to others as they journey towards faith is one of the great fruits of our time with Jesus. I pray that we can show someone the patience of Jesus today. We need his constant faithfulness. What a relief that we don't have to have it all figured out right away!

Prayer Starter: Do I expect God to fix me quickly? How can patience with myself help me to be patient with others?

PRIEST, PROPHET, KING

The Eucharist empowers us to cooperate in the work of salvation.

The Eucharist is a personal invitation to true, ongoing conversion. We are meant to be born again. In my role as a lay evangelist, I can be a part of another person's journey towards Christ, either through a serious word that I give, a comedic story that I tell, a song that I sing, or through the witness of my life.

Jesus welcomes the laborers and encourages them to come because the harvest is plentiful (Matthew 9:37). This call certainly extends to those in the ministerial priesthood, but it also includes the universal Church, because through our baptism in Christ, we are all now priest, prophet, and king. Think about this for a moment: the priest brings us Jesus, specifically in the sacraments, and the laypeople bring others to Christ by witnessing to God's grace in their lives. It isn't that the layperson is the end, nor the ministerial priest for that matter; rather, we are the willing means to the satisfactory end in Christ. We are not used in some objectified way but are invited to collaboratively participate in the saving work of Christ by leading and guiding.

When I bring my family to Jesus in the sacraments, I am fulfilling my role as priest, prophet, and king. When I speak a word or sing a song or invite strangers to look once more at Jesus' life, death, and resurrection, I am fulfilling my call to go and preach the gospel. When I pray unnoticed for the souls of the faithful departed or remember the struggling man or woman who has asked for my intercession, I am uniting my action with the saving acts of Jesus. While I am flawed, often distracted, sinful, and even disinterested at times, Jesus still invites me to be the priest, prophet, and king I am called to be through my baptism. Jesus wants conversion, in me and in those I will encounter this day. If I truly believe that Jesus is in the Eucharist and that he is, in fact, willingly asking for my involvement in sharing his love, then I must preach the good news even if my words come out awkwardly.

Moses felt that he was unable to be a great leader and a prophetic voice for God because he stuttered (Exodus 4:10). His past was messy; he certainly had a few skeletons in his closet. God saw all these flaws and called this man to become uncomfortable. Moses' inabilities were no match for God's profound possibilities, and the deliverance from Egypt demonstrated this fact unquestionably. God made Moses a great prophet who is still revered by many. His brother, Aaron, was a gift from God to assist in the articulation of his plan, and all that remained was for Moses to accept that he was the only one standing in the way of God's great work. Thankfully, he said yes to God's invitation.

Jeremiah was a young boy called to be a prophet for God. He felt unable to be the mouthpiece of the Lord because of his youth, and yet the Lord insisted that even while Jeremiah was still in his mother's womb, he had in fact been called to be the messenger of God's word (Jeremiah 1:4-10). The Lord gave Jeremiah the words to speak, and all that remained was for this young man to either accept or reject the call. The words Jeremiah would deliver would not be readily received, but in the end, Jeremiah was responsible only for obediently responding to God's call. He couldn't control the response of the Israelites.

Isaiah was another prophet who felt unfit for the task at hand. His struggle wasn't with youth or an inability to speak due to a speech impediment; rather, it was because of an acute awareness of his unclean lips (Isaiah 6:5). The encounter he had with God was a sobering moment of clarity for Isaiah, because not only was he unclean and unfit for such a holy call, but so also were the people to whom he would speak. God's fiery love purified Isaiah so that he could go and speak the word of God, and all that remained was his response. Isaiah said, "Here am I! Send me" (6:8).

There are numerous examples within Sacred Scripture that willingly point out the flaws of the called, yet in God's hand, the grace given does in fact meet the need of all involved. Jonah runs from his responsibilities, Sampson caves in to the seductions of Delilah, Elijah runs from Jezebel, and even Abraham attempts to fulfill God's promise in a rather unhelpful plan of action by sleeping with Hagar.

God is not afraid of our sin. He is not alarmed at our failures and inabilities because his plan includes provisions specifically addressing our weaknesses. All that remains is a response from a willing heart. The Eucharist is a personal invitation into true, ongoing conversion because it is the culmination of salvation history in the most effective way. Jesus in us does, in fact, change our hearts. Jesus in our lives now enables us to speak his word to those we encounter daily. The Eucharist is the Word now in us, consumed actually, readying us for the opposition we will face. This participation in the "sacrament of sacraments" enables us to offer as sacrifice our difficulties and joys as we miraculously participate in the redemptive work of Christ.

We are priests in Christ, and the Eucharistic sacrifice gives us a place to actually lay down our gifts. We are prophets in Christ, and with the Word of God in us, we can, with our spoken and lived lives, make an impact on the world in which we live. We are kings! "For he who is in you is greater than he who is in the world" (1 John 4:4), and it is time we realize that we can rule in a way that will help those in our reach. The Eucharist solidifies our baptismal grace because we encounter Jesus in the most intimate of ways: body, blood, soul, and divinity. The more we receive our Lord in the Eucharist, the more we will realize that we have been bought with a price (1 Corinthians 7:23) and that we are to be in the world but not of the world (John 17:14). We need a heart like David, a willingness like Isaiah, an offering like Abel, a passion like Elijah, a dedication like Noah, and a yes like Mary.

The Eucharist is Christ encountering us, asking us if we will be the word in this age, the message of hope in the hopelessness, and the light shining in the darkness. The Eucharist is Jesus uniting with us, inviting us to offer our troubles and cares, sins and sorrow, and joy and glories to him so that our lives can pour out with impact. The Eucharist is our Lord calling us to bring the world to him in our prayers and sacrifices, but we are also empowered to lead, guide, rescue, and care for those in our reach as a king does for his kingdom. We have been changed and continue to do so with each reception of Jesus at Mass. Come, Lord Jesus; we say yes to you today!

Prayer Starter: How am I fulfilling my baptismal call to be priest, prophet, and king?

RESPONDING TO DEATH

*Grounding our life in the Eucharist gives us
hope even in the face of death.*

The inevitability of death can cause us to respond in different ways. Some choose to entertain themselves regularly so that they never have to contemplate their mortality. Some choose to defy death by living on the edge, participating in extreme sports and daring expeditions and facing life with a seemingly defiant attitude that looks death in the face. A few are paralyzed with fear, assuming that every act or choice will bring their demise. We cannot in good conscience embrace these extremes: numbing avoidance, indifferent defiance, or paralytic immobility.

For the sinner and for the saint, there is a day coming in which we will leave this world for another. If we choose to believe that there is nothing facing us on the other side, then what we know and experience is all that is or will be. It is a sad state of affairs to find the end of life in view with no hope whatsoever of another journey that awaits us. There are two roads, and we choose one or the other every day: to believe there is something on the other side of the veil or not to believe.

But the fact that our lives have been truly grounded and resurrected in Christ Jesus and sustained by the Eucharist should give us a sense of hope in spite of death's looming approach. Our state of mind, then, should be quite different from someone who has resisted the invitation of the Spirit throughout his life. And if we can believe the stories of the saints who have articulated insights from the world to come, then we can attain a great sense of peace.

Some of the saints would write and reflect upon the meaning of life with a skull on their desks. This constant acknowledgment of death wasn't rooted in morbidity; rather, it grounded them in their mortality. Realizing that they were not immortal reminded them to live each day as if it were their last. Contemplating their mortality energized and enabled them to strive towards holiness, even when the odds were against them. Among the saints were martyrs like St. Polycarp. Refusing to compromise his faith to gain an extra day, month, or year of his life, he knew that each day was a gift from God and that the immortality that awaited him was of greater importance than living this life without integrity. The saints show us that life is far more valuable than we might have previously realized, and as a result, we must not carelessly pursue things that rob us of grace and purpose.

Prayer Starter: How can I live each day as if it were my last?

HEAVEN

We encounter a taste of heaven in every
Eucharistic feast.

Most small children have a fairly imaginative understanding of heaven. It likely involves mountains of ice cream, beloved animals, favorite toys, late evenings without bedtimes, and probably every video game ever created. The idea that heaven might be like church, however, seems to frighten kids, and probably most adults as well.

So what is heaven? I'd like to make this fairly simple, if I may. Heaven is our happiest moment, our favorite feeling, our best memory, our greatest joy, our sweetest day, but then multiplied infinitely. Heaven is not so much a location as the culmination of being in Christ. Heaven is the presence of God, and there is nothing about that which is boring.

Heaven is the greatest family gathering we could ever imagine. We celebrate the work and fruit of what God has done in and through us. Every good attribute we had here on earth is magnified in heaven. We won't be walking around in some sort of weird angelic daze, as if we can barely recognize our family and friends from that place called Earth. The struggles and sins, and the tears and fears within the family dynamic will be gone because we will be in the heavenly embrace, and all of the joys and intimate moments will be enjoyed to the utmost.

Heaven will be the constant surprise of God's love in the little and big things. The colors will be more intense, the music more amazing, the emotions richer, and the potential of imagination ever greater in the love of God.

And heaven is encountered in every Mass. We just don't have the emotions and clarity of senses necessary to reveal the fullness of what we are experiencing. For example, you can have a bad day and Jesus still gives himself to you at Mass. You cannot see the angels and saints, yet they are there. The foretaste of heaven given at Mass is the very presence of Jesus. All of heaven is present, but we often miss it because, as St. Paul says, we see things a bit dimly here (1 Corinthians 13:12). One day we will see him face-to-face, and, my friends, it will be such a beautiful surprise!

Prayer Starter: What has been my happiest moment in my life? How might heaven look like that?

the WORD
among us ®
The *Spirit* of Catholic Living